D1473711

KABBALAH
SIMPLY STATED

KABBALAH
SIMPLY STATED

A Conversation with the Rabbi

Paragon House
St. Paul, Minnesota

Published in the United States by
Paragon House
2285 University Avenue West
St. Paul, MN 55114

First Edition published 2003, Sinclair Books, London

Explanatory drawings which create a visual understanding
of Kabbalistic philosophy were graciously provided by artist
Nick Lombardo.

Library of Congress Cataloging-in-Publication Data

Waxman, Bob, 1956-
  Kabbalah simply stated : a conversation with the Rabbi / Bob
Waxman ; [illustrations by Phillip Ratner].-- 1st paragon ed.
      p. cm.
  Includes bibliographical references and index.
  ISBN 1-55778-842-1 (pbk. : alk. paper)
  1. Cabala. I. Ratner, Phillip. II. Title.

  BM525.W37 2004
  296.1'6--dc22
                                            2004011160

Manufactured in the United States of America
10 9 8 7 6 5 4 3 2 1

For current information about all releases from Paragon House,
visit the web site at http://www.paragonhouse.com

For Peggy, with love and appreciation.

Special thanks to Muriel Trachman who has been my guiding light of inspiration from the inception of this book to its completion. Muriel's unflinching optimism and relentless encouragement gave me no other choice but to write this book.

.

KABBALISTIC DREAMS

A Suite of Original Art Works Inspired by the Writings of the Kabbalah, the Zohar, and other Aspects of Mystical Judaism

The drawings in this book by Phillip Ratner were all created in the city of Safed, Israel where, according to tradition, Simon Ben-Yochai and his son received their mission. The artist chose black and white not only because those are the colors of the written Torah, but because they represent positive and negative energy and universal esoteric truths. Black and white still remains the purest form of visual communication.

All of these works are a cerebral rather that an intellectual interpretation of written passages. Years ago a close friend of the artist suggested that he sit with pencil and paper and meditate (Kavannah) on the Hebrew alphabet (which is the core of the Kabbalah) in order to see what might result. The artist was astonished to find symbolism that he had never used before and images set in a mystic atmosphere. The works all represent doors opening to nowhere or somewhere, chess boards that go through tunnels or are spread out like a carpet, small spheres connected to web-thin lines and clouds, suns and moons randomly placed.

In 1984, Ratner began devoting most of his energy into creating a permanent museum in Israel, The Israel Bible Museum. In 1999, The Dennis & Phillip Ratner Museum opened to the public in the Greater Washington, DC area, highlighting Ratner's Biblical work along with changing exhibitions of important contemporary artists.

The artist still continues to produce a rare few of these drawings each year and continues to create them sitting in his museum studio in the city of Safed overlooking the Sea of Galilee. Phillip Ratner has graciously allowed his work to be included here.

CONTENTS

A Message from the Rabbi

At the present time one of the most urgent needs is for the simplification of Kabbalistic teachings. Kabbalah should be made simple to understand. It is the fault of its exponents if it is made complicated, abstruse, or vague. Yet new students are always complaining that it is too difficult for them, and that their Biblical education has not been deep enough to enable them to understand it.

This is greatly the fault of Kabbalists who have taught Kabbalah in such a manner that new students sadly turn away from it. At classes, meetings, or when trying to interest the new student, it is absolutely useless to use unknown Hebrew words without their English translations. Nine times out of ten, it's due to laziness or conceit on the part of the teacher or facilitator.

The philosophy of Kabbalah should be mastered, and once that is done it is easy to express the most complex ideas in simple terms. Long drawn-out discussions about Ain-Soph and the details of the Spiritual Hierarchies are useless. Such ideas as Gilgul (journey of the soul), Neshamah (divine spark of God), Adam Kadmon (primordial man), the Sephirothal Tree (Tree of Life), the Tetragrammaton (Name of God), hidden messages in the Bible and the final cleaving to God (Devekut) should be the first subjects to put forward.

These concepts can all be expounded (if you have grasped the ideas and made them part of your thoughts) from a thousand different points of view. At all meetings the strongest effort should be made to simplify explanations by using English along with Hebrew to express the sacred philosophy of Kabbalah.

—Rabbi Azriel Abraham
June 1992

Abraham gazes at the stars in the sky.

INTRODUCTION

I was walking through Jerusalem one rainy afternoon when I saw a bookstore and decided to buy a book on Kabbalah. While I was standing on the checkout line, an elderly Rabbi approached me and asked me my name. I showed him my credit card and pointed to my name, and he said, "no, no, no, that was your name before—your new name is, Neer Aish-Donag." I asked him why he was so definite about this particular name, and he said, "just listen to me Neer, I see you're buying a book on Kabbalah, so trust me, you will be experiencing many life changing transformations from now on. You should start by changing your name."

The Rabbi and I sat down to have coffee and he said, "I've been studying Kabbalah for 60 years; please ask me any questions you want and I'll be happy to tell you what I know." First, I asked him if he wanted me to donate to his organization, and he said, "forget it—just buy me one of those big chocolate-chip cookies and a cup of decaf." So, I laughed, bought him what he wanted, and then I experienced the most memorable afternoon of my life.

I am sharing this dialogue with interested students of Kabbalah because Rabbi Abraham spoke directly from his heart. He had no hidden agenda and he started me on an incredible journey which continues to this day. I am deeply indebted to him for taking me under his wing and allowing me to be his student. He placed wisdom before dollars and gave love without conditions. He was truly a wise, pious, loving man, and I was extremely fortunate to have found such a wonderful teacher. This book is dedicated to my mentor and cherished friend, Rabbi Azriel Abraham.

—Bob Waxman
(Neer Aish-Donag)

Kabbalah—What's In A Name?

Neer: Rabbi, over the past few years, people of all faiths have become interested in Kabbalah.

Rabbi: (Laugh) Yes, everything old is new again. I've seen the rich and famous talking about Kabbalah on TV. If that's what it takes to spread the word about this sacred philosophy, then any news is good news.

Neer: So, can you set the record straight? What's the true definition of the word Kabbalah?

Rabbi: Well, I'm not a Hebrew version of Webster's Dictionary, but I'll give you the commonly accepted translation.

Neer: OK.

Rabbi: The word Kabbalah contains three Hebrew letters: KBL—literally, it means "tradition" or "to receive."

Neer: To receive what?

Rabbi: To receive the divine wisdom of God which has been passed down throughout the ages.

Neer: Please explain what you mean by "divine wisdom"?

Rabbi: OK, you want the long definition? I was trying to keep it short and sweet, but since you asked, I'll tell you. The goal of Kabbalah is to help you understand the hidden meanings of the Bible and the concealed mysteries of the Universe. Through Kabbalah you will uncover the deepest secrets of Life, Creation, and the Soul. You'll experience an incredible sense of illumination from within, and a greater understanding of your life's purpose. You will also discover the divine truth within yourself—and that truth, my friend—is the "divine wisdom" of God.

NEER: ...but what proof do we have that Kabbalah is truly God's wisdom?

RABBI: If you have any doubts, just give him a call—in fact, it's a local call here in Jerusalem (laugh).

NEER: That's a good one (laugh), but I'm not letting you off the hook that easily.

RABBI: OK, OK. What can I tell you? If a person only believes in God's wisdom after it has been proven, it's the same as saying, "I'll have faith when I no longer need faith, because now it's a scientific fact." Or it's like saying, "I'll believe in the infinite nature of God after it has been determined, witnessed and fully defined for my benefit as a finite thing." So, if a person will only accept the infinite wisdom of God in finite terms, they'll probably have to wait forever.

NEER: So, how will I know if Kabbalah is right for me?

RABBI: As you are introduced to Kabbalistic ideas, you will know if Kabbalah is right for you. If the teachings ring true within yourself, that should be proof enough. Your intuition will always guide you toward the true wisdom of God.

NEER: So, can anyone study Kabbalah?

RABBI: Of course. All you need is a curious mind and an open heart.

NEER: ...but, aren't there strict rules that must be obeyed?

RABBI: There is no dogma in Kabbalah. In fact, there are no rules at all. All you need is a willingness to learn.

NEER: ...but, aren't new students required to accept all Kabbalistic teachings?

RABBI: Absolutely not. You study what you like, and you leave the rest for another time.

NEER: Now, that's a relief.

RABBI: I think most people are very careful about accepting new spiritual ideas. There's no pressure, no time schedule, and no one to judge you when you study Kabbalah.

NEER: ...and there's no guilt, no fear, no sin, and no eternal damnation?

RABBI: (Laugh) Hardly, unless you choose to impose those ideas upon yourself, which I wouldn't recommend by the way (smile).

NEER: Now, why is Kabbalah also spelled with a "C" and a "Q"?

RABBI: It's spelled many different ways depending on who's interpreting it. The traditional Jewish spelling is Kabbalah, or Kabalah with a "K". Cabala with a "C" refers to Christian Cabala. Qabala with a "Q" is associated with the Hermetic or Egyptian tradition.

NEER: So, who has the right interpretation of Kabbalah?

RABBI: (Laugh) You're funny. That's like asking who knows the right way to cook a chicken. Accepting a religious philosophy is strictly subjective. If anyone tells you they have the right path for you—turn around and run as fast as you can.

NEER: I see your point.

Rabbi: Good. I'm glad you are a logical person (laugh).

Neer: Thank you, and my Mother knows the right way to cook a chicken (laugh).

Rabbi: (Laugh) Well, of course she does! And I always like a man who defends his Mother's chicken!

FROM WHENCE DOES IT COME?

NEER: Rabbi, what books are studied when learning Kabbalah?

RABBI: There are many, but the most popular ones are: The Book of Light *(Sepher Bahir)*, which includes ancient writings about Ezekiel's Chariot; The Book of Formation *(Sepher Yetzirah)*, which introduces the *Sephirot* and the Tree of Life; and The Book of Splendor *(Zohar)*, which is an expression of the most profound philosophies ever written relating to the innermost secrets of the Soul.

NEER: ...and who wrote these books?

RABBI: Even the greatest scholars don't know for sure, but there's credible evidence all three books include ancient, oral wisdom teachings. The great Rabbi's like Maimonides, Isaac the Blind, Moses De Leon and Moses Cordorvero began interpreting and writing down 'the Oral Tradition' between 1170 CE and 1570 CE. This was the golden era of Kabbalistic thought.

NEER: ...and what part did Moses of the Bible play in all this?

RABBI: That's a good question. According to the Bible, Moses was raised in Pharaoh's court as a "Prince of Egypt", so he would have been familiar with the teachings of the Egyptian Mystery Schools. So, the real question is, did Moses incorporate his esoteric, or hidden knowledge, into the teachings of ancient Kabbalah? And the answer is: there's a 99 percent probability that he did.

NEER: Do you recognize any similarities between Egyptian philosophy and Kabbalah?

FROM WHENCE DOES IT COME ?

POSSIBILITY #1:

MOSES ON MT.SINAI

POSSIBILITY #2:

KABBALISTIC EVOLUTION

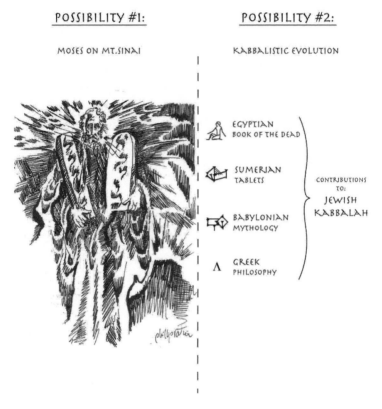

EGYPTIAN
BOOK OF THE DEAD

SUMERIAN
TABLETS

CONTRIBUTIONS
TO:
JEWISH
KABBALAH

BABYLONIAN
MYTHOLOGY

GREEK
PHILOSOPHY

Three Primary Kabbalistic Texts:
1) The Sepher Bahir (Book of Light)
2) The Sepher Yetzirah (Book of Formation)
3) The Zohar (Book of Splendor)

RABBI: Yes, especially the writings on the eternal validity of the Soul. The Egyptians were fascinated with the after-life and the Soul's journey to higher levels of existence. Kabbalah has assimilated many of these philosophical influences over the centuries.

NEER: ...and where else do these philosophical influences come from?

RABBI: Besides Egypt? Sumeria, Babylonia, Persia, Greece and many other civilizations who intermingled with the Jewish people.

NEER: So, can you give me an example of a famous philosopher who influenced Kabbalistic writers?

RABBI: If you read essays by Plato (427 BCE), Philo (25 BCE), Plotinus (204 CE), and Proclus (411 CE), you'll find interesting references relating to the eternal nature of the Soul, the relationship between spiritual ideas and mathematics, and how man is an exact replica of everything that exists in the Universe. All these topics are found in the later writings of Kabbalah.

NEER: ...but, how do we know, who influenced who? Maybe Plato and these other philosophers were influenced by Kabbalah?

RABBI: It's a good question, but Plato was writing in 400 BCE. His ideas didn't show up in Kabbalistic literature until 1150 CE, which was just about the same time Plato's manuscripts were being translated into other languages.

NEER: So, there's Greek philosophy in Kabbalah?

RABBI: In my opinion? Definitely. Philo and Josephus were

Jewish historians and big fans of Plato. Philo tried to form a new religion combining Judaism and Greek philosophy, but it didn't work out very well.

NEER: Why not?

RABBI: The Greeks didn't want to give up their gods, and adult men didn't want to be circumcised.

NEER: Ouch! I can understand the second reason for sure.

RABBI: ...and there was another reason why Philo failed. His new religion was based on logic instead of love.

NEER: So, is love the basis of Kabbalah?

RABBI: Absolutely! "Thou shalt love the Lord thy God, with all thy heart, with all thy Soul, and with all thy might." And Kabbalah tells us, "The Lord thy God" exists inside each and every one of us. So, we must learn to love this spark of God within ourselves. You certainly can't love others until you've learned to love your own divine essence.

THE SOUL'S RELIGION: TRUTH

NEER: Rabbi, is Kabbalah mostly for Jewish people?

RABBI: Absolutely not! Kabbalah is for anyone who believes in unity, love, and compassion. But, there are people who believe some Souls are different than other Souls.

NEER: Well, are they?

RABBI: Of course not. The entire philosophy falls apart if we accept this premise. Kabbalah teaches that ALL Souls come from One Universal Divine Source. In other words, we are all sparks from the same fire.

NEER: Or droplets from the same ocean?

RABBI: Exactly. Now, some people believe one ocean is separate from another, but the truth is, each ocean overflows into the next. So there's really just one big ocean.

NEER: And the same holds true for Souls?

RABBI: Yes, but some people will insist the Pacific Ocean is separate from the Atlantic.

NEER: A Californian and a New Yorker might think so (laugh)!

RABBI: And that's exactly my point! Just as some people believe "their" Ocean is separate from another, some people believe "their" Souls are separate from other Souls. This type of thinking just divides people and doesn't serve any purpose.

NEER: So, all Souls are made of the same "stuff"?

RABBI: That's right. There is only One God and we are ALL God's children.

NEER: So, God doesn't belong to any one particular religion? (laugh).

RABBI: There's not one word in any religious scripture indicating that God is a dues paying member of any religious organization (laugh).

NEER: Good one (laugh). Now, why are the Jews referred to in the Bible as "the chosen people"?

RABBI: Well, the real question is, what were the Jewish people chosen for?

NEER: OK, if that's the real question, then what's the real answer?

RABBI: The Jewish people were "chosen" to deliver the message of monotheism to the world; which we've done quite well by the way. Today, all three "western" religions practice and accept the fundamental law of monotheism.

NEER: I understand. Now, how is God in Kabbalah different from God of the Bible?

RABBI: Now that, my friend is a very good question, so let's start—literally—"In the Beginning."

AIN-SOPH USING ASPECTS OF ITSELF
TO CREATE AN OCEAN:

• SPACE • MOTION • DURATION

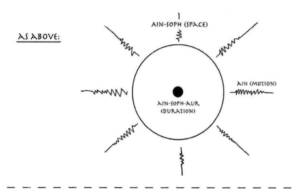

AS ABOVE:

AIN-SOPH (SPACE)

AIN (MOTION)

AIN-SOPH-AUR
(DURATION)

- -

BIRTH OF AN OCEAN

SO BELOW:

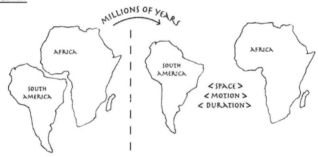

MILLIONS OF YEARS

AFRICA

SOUTH
AMERICA

SOUTH
AMERICA

AFRICA

< SPACE >
< MOTION >

GOD OF KABBALAH: AIN-SOPH
(EN-SOF, EIN-SOPH, EYN-SOF ETC.)

RABBI: For simplicity sake, let's say God in Kabbalah is infinite, incomprehensible and unspeakable.

NEER: Well, if God is unspeakable, how do we use words to speak about IT?

RABBI: We don't. We can only say that God or Ain-Soph is: "Everything That Is, That Was and Shall Be."

NEER: So, where's the King with the long beard, sitting on his Throne surrounded by singing angels?

RABBI: You'll find him in the Bible, and he's a very comforting image for many people. But in Kabbalah, God is an abstract concept of Being and Non-Being. Ain-Soph can only be symbolized by Space, Motion and Duration BEFORE the existence of the Universe.

NEER: All right, hold on now, you're getting into all that metaphysical stuff.

RABBI: OK then, let's keep it simple. Let's go back to your metaphor of an ocean.

NEER: OK.

RABBI: Now, an ocean doesn't appear out of thin air. There must be some form of divine architecture behind it—agreed?

NEER: Makes sense.

RABBI: So, what does an ocean need to become an ocean? It needs Space to exist, Motion for expansion, and Duration to have the experience of being an ocean.

AIN-SOPH

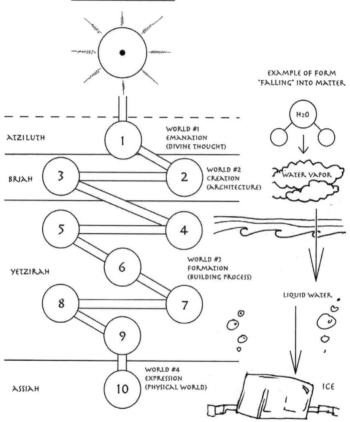

EXAMPLE OF FORM "FALLING" INTO MATTER

ATZILUTH

1 WORLD #1 EMANATION (DIVINE THOUGHT)

BRIAH

3 **2** WORLD #2 CREATION (ARCHITECTURE)

5 **4**

6 WORLD #3 FORMATION (BUILDING PROCESS)

YETZIRAH

8 **7**

9

ASSIAH

10 WORLD #4 EXPRESSION (PHYSICAL WORLD)

H₂O

WATER VAPOR

LIQUID WATER

ICE

NEER: So, how does this relate to God?

RABBI: Well, doesn't it make sense that God would use aspects of ITSELF to create an ocean? or a planet? or a Universe? Space, Motion, and Duration—these are the vital ingredients.

NEER: So, God uses aspects of ITSELF to build the Universe and everything in it?

RABBI: That's right, and there are four levels of reality used in this building process.

NEER: So, Kabbalah teaches multi-dimensional layers of reality?

RABBI: Yes. There are Four Worlds of Existence, and we can see them right here on Earth.

NEER: We can?

RABBI: Yes. Let's continue with your water motif. We know that water exists in four different states: atoms, vapor, liquid and solids.

NEER: OK.

RABBI: Now, as $H2O$ changes to vapor, then to liquid, and then to ice, we can see its form becoming harder.

NEER: I'm following you.

RABBI: So, the same holds true for all types of forms. They fall into physical matter, just as Adam—mythologically speaking—fell to Earth from the Garden of Eden.

NEER: So, how does Adam's fall correspond to different forms of water?

RABBI: Adam's atoms fell from the Third World of shadows to the Fourth World of the flesh. Correspondingly, the liquidity of water falls into a hardened state of ice.

NEER: ...and what are these Worlds called?

RABBI: World Three is called Yetzirah—the World of Formation. World Four is Assiah—the World of Expression.

NEER: And what about Worlds One and Two?

RABBI: World One is Atziluth—the World of Emanation. This is where God thinks about all that is yet to come. In Briah, or World Two, his builders—the Elohim—get to work and begin the creative process.

NEER: ...and who are the Elohim ?

RABBI: They are divine aspects of the Godhead.

NEER: Huh?

RABBI: OK, think of it like this: at a certain moment, Ain-Soph reflects ITSELF into something finite. This is called the Godhead. It occupies the top spot on the Tree of Life, and eventually, it unfolds into nine divine aspects. Got it?

NEER: I think so.

RABBI: Now, think of the Godhead as a clear prism.

NEER: OK.

RABBI: Imagine a brilliant white light shining through this prism and the light separating into various colors, sounds and vibrations.

NEER: ...and then what happens?

RABBI: These rays of light, or Elohim, begin building a new physical Universe.

NEER: ...and does the Godhead give them a deadline to finish their job?

RABBI: Yes, six cosmic days, and on the seventh day they rest.

NEER: So, this is the creation story of Genesis with a slight twist?

RABBI: A huge twist. You see, before the Beginning, there was a resting period from a former Universe which had come to an end. This Universe of ours is not the first, nor will it be the last.

NEER: So, how does the Beginning actually begin?

RABBI: Well, when the hour strikes, a cosmic alarm goes off, and a new Beginning moves into action. From that point on, the Godhead acts like a lightening bolt and IT descends into matter. When IT reaches the tenth or lowest sphere, our dense physical Universe comes into being.

NEER: And which ancient text explains the Godhead's descension into matter?

RABBI: In the *Sepher Yetzirah*, the Godhead gives birth to nine emanations as IT descends into matter. Now, as IT unfolds, IT expresses ITSELF at each level of reality.

NEER: But if there are only Four Worlds, how does the Godhead unfold into nine aspects?

RABBI: Good question. There are Four Worlds of Existence, and each World contains a different number of spheres or Sephirot. These ten spheres represent the Godhead or Keter, plus ITS nine emanations. If you look at the Tree of Life, you'll see the Sephira Keter in World One. In World Two, there are two Sephirot. In World Three there are six Sephirot and in World Four there's only one Sephira, called Malkuth or the Kingdom.

NEER: Wow, that's a lot of information to swallow.

RABBI: Yes, a lot to swallow, and a lot to digest, my friend (smile).

Neer: Which brings us to the subject of reincarnation.

Rabbi: If you'd like to call it that.

Neer: OK, what's the official Kabbalistic term for the return of the Soul?

Rabbi: Transmigration, along with the underlying theory of Metempsychosis.

Neer: For simplicity sake, can we just use the word reincarnation?

Rabbi: We could, but there is a difference.

Neer: OK, please explain.

Rabbi: The word reincarnation is defined by the Eastern religions as a series of births and rebirths. In Kabbalah, the doctrine of Transmigration or Gilgul, is mentioned first in the *Sepher Bahir* (12th Century CE) and is described as a form of punishment for those who didn't obey the First Commandment. But, Moses De Leon, the author of the *Zohar*, didn't like this idea of punishing the Soul, so he defined Transmigration as "the pursuit of perfecting the Soul during its time on Earth."

Neer: That's a very good explanation.

Rabbi: Now, as for Metempsychosis, this doctrine refers to the life essence as it gains experience in each of the four kingdoms on Earth. First, it gains experience as a mineral, then a plant, then an animal, and finally, it blossoms into a human Soul.

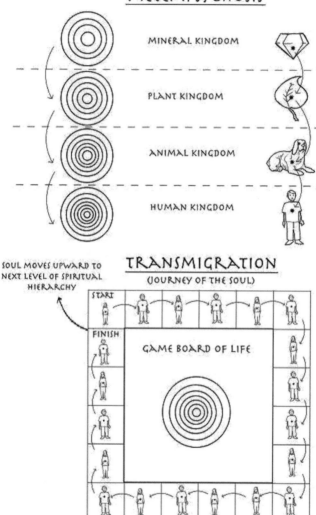

NEER: So, I was a plant once upon a time?

RABBI: No, YOU were not a plant, but the essence of your life-force was. Once upon a time, your instinctual nature traveled through the mineral, plant and animal kingdoms. From there, your life-force gave birth to your mind, and then your human experience began.

NEER: Now, do you think Darwin would have agreed with this theory of evolution?

RABBI: Probably. It's the spiritual equivalent of Darwin's theory of evolution.

NEER: …and what's the basis for this spiritual theory?

RABBI: If you looked at x-rays of the four different stages of a woman's pregnancy, you would see four different shapes quite clearly. First, you'd see a round mineral-like object, then a globular plant-like thing, then an animal-like tadpole with a tail, and finally, the shape of a human embryo emerges. This is the theory of Metempsychoses in snap-shot form.

NEER: So, God gives us clues in the physical world to help us understand the spiritual world?

RABBI: All we have to do is pay attention.

NEER: So, how does an animal become a human?

RABBI: Well, Darwin said our bodies evolved from the Animal Kingdom and then progressed into the Human Kingdom. So, we can apply this same theory to spiritual evolution.

NEER: OK.

FOUR STAGES OF BIRTH

STAGE #1
(MINERAL)

STAGE #2
(PLANT)

STAGE #3
(ANIMAL)

STAGE #4
(HUMAN)

RABBI: There comes a time when man realizes he can make his own choices. His natural instinct becomes secondary to his free will. Well, at that point he becomes a self-conscious being. Remember God's famous words from Exodus, "I AM THAT I AM"? Notice, when you say these words out loud, you're expressing your own awareness of yourself.

NEER: So, when I say, "I am," I really mean, I know that I'm me?

RABBI: That's right. Descartes said he could only prove one axiom, "I think, therefore I am." But, he still couldn't prove what gave him the ability to think. The fact is, as smart as we are, we still don't know—how we know.

NEER: So, Kabbalah gives us the answer?

RABBI: Yes. Our ability "to know" comes from two parts of our Soul—Ruach and Neshamah. Ruach is the seat of our spiritual awareness, and Neshamah is our divine spark of God.

NEER: ...and, these two parts of our Soul create self-consciousness?

RABBI: Yes, it makes sense, doesn't it?

NEER: Rabbi, my divine spark is on overdrive, thanks to you!

RABBI: That's very good news. Now, there is a third part of the Soul called Nephesh, which is the breath of life, but we'll get to that later.

NEER: That's fine with me. Now, can we return to the subject of reincarnation?

RABBI: Sure. When man becomes a thinking being, his Soul cannot return to the Animal Kingdom or below. There is always a forward progression. Just as physical man cannot devolve back into an ape, spiritual man cannot devolve back into the consciousness of a donkey. So, the Soul is always moving forward from lifetime to lifetime.

NEER: In other words, someone who graduates from college isn't going back to high school?

RABBI: That's right. It wouldn't make any sense to go backward since the entire cosmos is always moving forward. It's all part of that continuous Motion we were talking about.

NEER: I understand. Now, what happens to the Soul after a lifetime has ended?

RABBI: The Soul enters a higher state of consciousness where it rests and recharges its batteries.

NEER: I can relate to that. I think my batteries need recharging right now!

RABBI: Good, that's very good. That means I'm doing my job (smile).

NEER: Rabbi, please tell me about the Tree of Life and the ten spheres?

RABBI: They are called the ten Sephirot, or individually— Sephira. They form the Sephirothal Tree of Life. The Sephirot symbolize divine attributes and every aspect of our existence. The Tree of Life is one of the most important frameworks in Kabbalah. We find it first in the ancient text, the *Sepher Yetzirah*.

NEER: …and why is the Tree of Life so important?

RABBI: The Sephirothal Tree explains how the Godhead unfolds and how everything in the Universe came into being.

NEER: Can you give me an example?

RABBI: Sure. Let's look at the Ten Commandments.

NEER: OK.

RABBI: The First Commandment relates to pure Spirit. As you say it out loud—listen to yourself. You are stating your belief that "I Am" or You/Yourself are a divine spark of God: "I Am the Lord Thy God and Thou Shalt Have No Other Gods Before Me."

NEER: So, when I say "I" and "Me," I'm really saying God and I are one?

RABBI: Yes, because you come from God and you will return to God. So, you and God are truly one.

NEER: So, how does the First Commandment relate to the Sephirothal Tree?

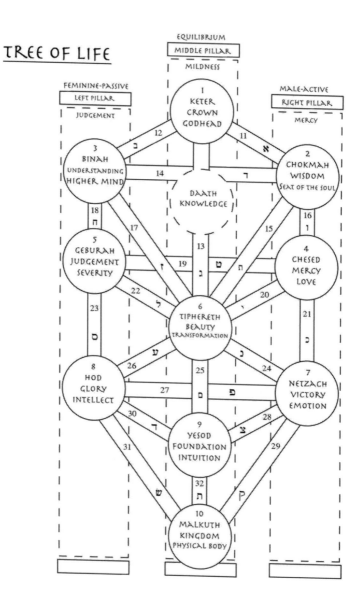

TREE OF LIFE

RABBI: The First Commandment speaks only of pure Spirit and so does the first Sephira Keter. By matching-up the Ten Commandments with the ten descending Sephirot, we can see a direct corresponding relationship between the two.

NEER: So, each Sephira represents an essential quality of each Commandment?

RABBI: That's right. Now, the last Commandment speaks only of matter, and it warns us not to covet our neighbor's possessions.

NEER: So, there's a change in emphasis from Spirit to matter?

RABBI: Yes, the First Commandment and first Sephira relate only to Spirit, and the last Commandment and last Sephira relate only to matter. So, here we can see the fall from Spirit to matter on the Sephirothal Tree.

NEER: That example works very well using the Commandments.

RABBI: ...and, the Sephirot can also "map-out" just about any subject you can think of. Even a baseball team with a designated hitter can be plotted out.

NEER: Interesting. So, how does the Sephirothal Tree relate to me?

RABBI: Good question. It can transform you into a divine being as you climb the ladder of life.

NEER: ...and does this "ladder" have any connection to Jacob's Ladder?

RABBI: Yes, you've hit a bull's eye. Now think for a moment: where was Jacob when he dreamt about that ladder

reaching up into the heavens?

NEER: Wasn't he in the desert?

RABBI: Correct, and whenever a Biblical figure goes wandering through the desert, it usually means one thing.

NEER: ...and that is?

RABBI: A transformation is about to take place.

NEER: So, Jacob was on the verge of a personal transformation?

RABBI: Yes.

NEER: ...and how does Jacob's transformation relate to The Tree of Life?

RABBI: Well, Jacob is a universal symbol for Man at the crossroads of life. He is the human condition; he's the Everyman. He lies to his father, loves his mother, deceives his brother, works hard for his uncle, marries two jealous sisters, acquires massive wealth, and has 12 boys and a girl.

NEER: He must have been very stressed-out.

RABBI: ...and on top of that, his brother Esau wanted to kill him.

NEER: Oh gosh, why?

RABBI: ...because Jacob stole his birthright to become the leader of the new Jewish nation.

NEER: So, that's why he escaped into the desert?

RABBI: Yes, Jacob was being hunted down by Esau, and one night he went to sleep and dreamt of a ladder reach-

ing up to the heavens, and then....

NEER: ...don't tell me—God appears.

RABBI: Right on cue, and God tells Jacob in the dream, he
         must build a new nation and continue the work of his
         Father Isaac and Grandfather Abraham.

NEER: Just like a family business being handed down from
         one generation to the next?

RABBI: Yes, except this was the business of starting a new na-
         tion and a new religion.

NEER: So where does the Tree of Life fit into all this?

RABBI: Let's take a look. Jacob is the main character in the
         story. He begins his spiritual journey at the bottom of
         the Tree of Life in Sphere #10, or Malkuth. This is
         the lowest level of spiritual awareness. He moves up
         to Sphere #9, or Yesod, when his intuition leads him
         into the desert.

NEER: ...and doesn't Jacob wrestle with an Angel?

RABBI: Yes, and he prevails. Jacob was really wrestling with
         his own conscience, and after his "dark night of the
         Soul," he finds redemption by overcoming his lower
         nature. On the Sephirothal Tree, he balances the op-
         posing Sephirot Geburah (severity) and Chesed (mer-
         cy), and moves into the Sephira Tiphereth (beauty),
         where he is transformed into a Patriarch.

NEER: OK, and what about the other Sephirot? What do
         they symbolize?

RABBI: They represent all the aspects of ourselves which
         must be in balance. Sphere #4, or Chesed, represents

the love and compassion we have for others. Sphere #5—Geburah or Din, reflects our severe, critical judgment of ourselves and others. Sphere #7, or Netzach, is our emotional nature. Sphere #8, or Hod, is our logical side and intellect. Jacob experiences all these Spheres and finally arrives in Sphere #6, or Tiphereth. There he finds balance, beauty and transformation. So, in Tiphereth, Jacob is transformed into a humble servant of God, and a new name is bestowed upon him....

NEER: ...wait a minute...I know this one...he was given the name Israel.

RABBI: That's right, "he who strives with God." So, when Jacob lands in Tiphereth, he forms a direct connection with the Godhead.

NEER: ...and, in Tiphereth, the "God within" is set free to join forces with the "God above."

RABBI: That's right, and in Tiphereth we become true sons and daughters of God.

NEER: Sounds like a nice place to be.

RABBI: There's no better place, my friend.

Daath—Not Quite a Sephira

NEER: Rabbi, what's this dotted sphere in the center column of the Tree?

RABBI: Oh, that's Daath, it means knowledge.

NEER: ...and why is it "dotted-in"?

RABBI: Because it's not a Sephira.

NEER: Then, what is it?

RABBI: It's known as the Abyss. It connects the three higher aspects of the Tree with the seven lower qualities. Daath is the bridge between the spiritual world of God, and our physical world of duality.

NEER: When you say "duality," what do you mean?

RABBI: Duality begins when spirit and matter are bound together. These are the necessary ingredients to form a physical universe. We see duality in hot and cold, life and death, north and south, positive and negative, male and female, and so on. Our world has a dual nature forming opposites which are intricately woven together. However, in the purely spiritual world beyond the Universe, matter doesn't exist—so there's no duality.

NEER: So, Daath connects these two worlds?

RABBI: Yes, it's the connecting link between the metaphysical and the physical.

NEER: So, why is it defined as knowledge?

RABBI: Because, Daath is used as a vehicle for the God's knowledge as it crosses the Abyss between the two Worlds of Briah and Yetzirah. Daath is also the main pipeline between the Sephira Binah and the Sephira Chesed on the Tree of Life.

NEER: ...and what type of knowledge is God transmitting down this pipeline?

RABBI: First, the "All-Knowingness" of Keter descends into the Divine Wisdom of Chokmah, which is then transformed into the Understanding of Binah. Then this Divine Understanding crosses the Abyss through Daath and is converted into the love and mercy of Chesed. From there, the descension of divine attributes continues all the way down to the tenth Sephira—Malkuth.

NEER: So, Daath is like an express mail service between God and mankind?

RABBI: Yes, that's a good analogy, and it's carrying precious cargo—divine wisdom.

NEER: ...and its final destination is?

RABBI: Our hearts and minds – but, only if we decide to open the package.

NEER: Ah, but sometimes those express packages are hard to open.

RABBI: Don't worry my friend, I'll be happy to help you open that very special package anytime you want (smile).

NEER: You already are Rabbi, you already are (smile).

THE CHARIOT

NEER: Rabbi, why do Kabbalists always talk about the Chariot?

RABBI: Oh, you mean the Merkabah; that's the contraption Ezekiel wrote about.

NEER: ...and what kind of contraption was it?

RABBI: Well, rather than repeat the Biblical description of this strange flying machine, why don't we talk about how it relates to Kabbalah.

NEER: Good idea.

RABBI: You see, some Kabbalists believe Ezekiel's mystical vision was the historical starting point of modern Kabbalah.

NEER: But, don't others say that the Kabbalah was given to Moses on Mt. Sinai?

RABBI: I wasn't there, so I can't say for sure (laugh). Yes, that's one theory, and there are many others. However, we know from Biblical historians that a group of Rabbis known as the Merkabah Mystics studied the Book of Ezekiel and the symbolism of the Chariot.

NEER: ...and during what time period did this take place?

RABBI: The Merkabah Mystics appeared in the first century CE. They developed a mystical philosophy from ancient books such as Genesis, Elijah, Ezekiel and Enoch.

NEER: All the strange stuff, eh?

RABBI: Yes, philosophers seem to gravitate toward the "strange stuff," and thanks to Ezekiel, they had all the strange stuff they would ever need in one lifetime.

THE MERKABAH (EZEKIEL'S CHARIOT)

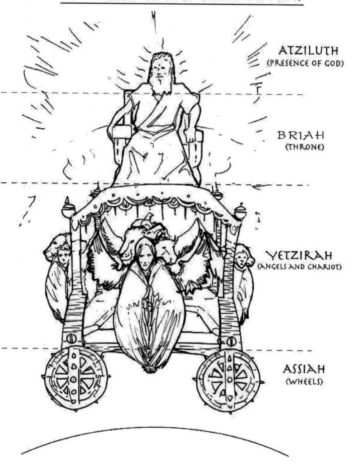

ATZILUTH
(PRESENCE OF GOD)

BRIAH
(THRONE)

YETZIRAH
(ANGELS AND CHARIOT)

ASSIAH
(WHEELS)

NEER: So, maybe Ezekiel was having a bad dream when he saw this Chariot?

RABBI: Maybe...or maybe he was having a real encounter with God. He describes a Chariot of Fire falling from the sky. In the center of the Chariot, there were four figures and each figure had four faces: a human, a lion, an ox and an eagle.

NEER: ...and where was God when the Chariot came flying by?

RABBI: His "Presence" was sitting on top of the Chariot. Below his face, Ezekiel saw his beard, the throne, angels, faces, and wheels.

NEER: So, what does Kabbalah say about this "Close Encounter of the Third Kind" (laugh)?

RABBI: Let's start with the faces. They symbolize four signs of the Zodiac. The lion is Leo, the human is Aquarius, the ox or bull is Taurus, and the eagle is Scorpio.

NEER: I thought the scorpion was the symbol of Scorpio.

RABBI: It is today, but in ancient times it was the eagle.

NEER: That's interesting. So, why did Ezekiel write about astrology?

RABBI: Ezekiel wanted us to know that ancient astrologers were keeping track of cosmic time. The four constellations mentioned by Ezekiel are: Leo, Aquarius, Taurus and Scorpio. They are also known as the four *fixed points* of the Zodiac.

NEER: So, Ezekiel was giving us a map of the stars?

THE FOUR FIXED POINTS OF THE ZODIAC

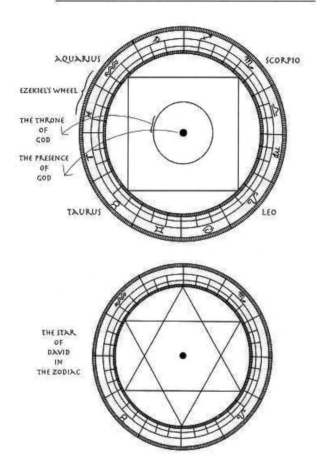

RABBI: Yes, and now it gets really interesting. You see, the
         Sun completes its own elliptical orbit every 25,920
         years. So, when we divide this number by the twelve
         constellations, it tells us we are passing through each
         constellation every 2,160 years.

NEER: ...and which constellation are we in now?

RABBI: According to Ezekiel's Chariot, we are moving out of
         the Age of Pisces and into the Age of Aquarius. Ezekiel
         was telling us that each Age of the Zodiac was split into
         three parts. He wanted people to know which third of
         the 2,160 time-span they were living in.

NEER: ...and why is that so important?

RABBI: Because most major world events tend to occur at the
         beginning, middle and end of each Zodiacal Age.

NEER: They do?

RABBI: Yes, as King Solomon tell us in Ecclesiastes, "there's
         a time for every purpose under heaven." So, here's
         the Kabbalistic key—everything moves in cycles—
         there's always a time of creation, a time of progres-
         sion and a time of decay.

NEER: Now, that's intriguing. Can you give me an example?

RABBI: Sure. Abraham is associated with the creative phase
         of Aries.

NEER: ....and how do we know that?

RABBI: The Bible tells us that Abraham—formerly Abram—
         sacrificed a ram instead of his son Isaac. The ram is
         the symbol of the Age of Aries, and the Hebrew let-
         ter Hé also symbolizes Aries. God added the Hé to

CHRONOLOGY OF THE AGE OF ARIES (SYMBOL—THE KAM)

PHASE #1

CREATION
TIME CIRCA 2,160 B.C.E.—ABRAM SPEAKS TO GOD IN GENESIS.
GOD CHANGES HIS NAME TO ABRAHAM.
ABRAHAM SACRIFICES RAM INSTEAD OF HIS SON ISAAC.
BEGINNING OF THE AGE

PHASE #2

PROGRESSION
TIME CIRCA 1,440 B.C.E.—MOSES PRESERVES MONOTHEISM.
MOSES DESTROYS GOLDEN CALF REPRESENTING THE EGYPTIAN AGE
OF TAURUS THE BULL (4,320 B.C.E.–2,160 B.C.E.
MIDDLE OF THE AGE

PHASE #3

DECAY
TIME 720 B.C.E.—NORTHERN KINGDOM OF ISRAEL DESTROYED.
TIME 586 B.C.E.—FIRST TEMPLE DESTROYED.
TIME 70 C.E.—SECOND TEMPLE DESTROYED.
END OF THE AGE

DAWNING OF THE AGE OF PISCES

Abram's name, and thus he became Abraham. Then, God gave the letter Hé to Abraham's wife Sarai, and she became Sarah.

NEER: So, the Hé represents their direct connection to God during the Age of Aries.

RABBI: Yes, and when you look at the Tree of Life, you'll see the letter Hé is path #15 which connects Chokmah (God's Wisdom) to Tiphereth (Man's Divine Spark). Path #15 can also be broken down to: $1+5=6$, and 6 brings us right back to Sephira #6 associated with Tiphereth.

NEER: Now, that's truly fascinating.

RABBI: Of course it is, and to make it more fascinating, the letter Hé symbolizes the Age of Aries. The first third, or "creative phase" of Aries, began in 2,160 BCE with Abraham. The second third, or "progressive phase", started with Moses in 1440 BCE. The last third, or "decaying phase" began with the Assyrian invasion of Israel in the year 720 BCE. Now, please take note of the 720 year interval between each phase.

NEER: Right, and the number 720 rings a bell for some reason?

RABBI: Because if you drop the zero, you have the number 72.

NEER: ...as in the 72 names of God?

RABBI: Yes, and some of these names relate to Creation, others to Progression and some to Decay. Once again, a beginning, a middle and an end.

NEER: ...and that sounds just like the cycle of human life. We're born, we live, and we die.

philip vatnes

Rabbi: That's right.

Neer: So, the number 72 symbolizes all three phases of life?

Rabbi: Yes, and life itself. 72 is $7+2=9$, and 9 is the number of months needed to create a human life. Also, the number 18 is the value of Chai or "Life"; and $1+8=9$. Nine is the only number which contains all the other numbers.

Neer: How so?

Rabbi: If you add $0+1+2+3+4+5+6+7+8+9$, the total is: 45 and $4+5=9$. So, the number 9 is the container of all the numbers in the finite Universe. Now, when the Star of David is placed inside the Tree of Life, the six points of the Star touch nine Sephirot. The top point touches Keter and the bottom point touches the 9th Sephira, Yesod. Now, Yesod is the sphere of Earthly Paradise, or Eden, and it connects directly to the Godhead, or Keter. In Kabbalistic numerology, or Gematria, the Man who occupies Eden is Adam of the dust. His Hebrew name is spelled: Aleph (1) + Daleth (4) + Mem (40) = 45, and once again, $4+5=9$. So, 9 is the number of Adam or Man; and Man is the container of all the elements in the Universe. Got it?

Neer: Yes, point well taken—nine is THE number. And now I understand why a cat has 9 lives (smile).

Rabbi: (Laugh) Yes, and "a stitch in time, saves nine" and so on.

Neer: So, getting back to Ezekiel, what part did he play in this cosmic drama?

RABBI: He played a big part. Ezekiel knew the third phase of Aries had begun in 720 BCE, which was the final phase of decay. The Assyrians took control of Israel, ten of the twelve tribes of Israel disappeared, and the Feminine Presence of God, known as Shekinah, went off into exile.

NEER: And why did the Jews believe the Shekinah was exiled?

RABBI: When the Assyrians conquered Israel, they filled the First Temple with Assyrian Gods, so the Shekinah no longer had a dwelling place. When the Jews were exiled, so was the Shekinah.

NEER: ….and what happened next?

RABBI: In 586 BCE, the First Temple was destroyed and Ezekiel's famous vision of the Merkabah occurred.

NEER: …and besides the astrological significance, what other message was Ezekiel trying to convey?

RABBI: Ezekiel wanted to revive the spirit of Judaism, and he was delivering God's message of hope. The time had come for the Jews to renew their faith in God, build a Second Temple, and revitalize the nation of Israel.

NEER: …and when was the Temple rebuilt?

RABBI: In 515 BCE the Second Temple was built and the Shekinah found a new home.

NEER: …and how long did the Second Temple last?

RABBI: The Second Temple was destroyed in 70 CE. This marked the end of the Age of Aries and the completion of the 2,160 Zodiacal cycle.

NEER: ...and after Aries, what Age came next?

RABBI: The new Age of Pisces was ushered in.

NEER: ...and are we still in the Age of Pisces now?

RABBI: Yes, we're at the very end of the Piscean Age. Or, to say it another way: "This is the dawning of the Age of Aquarius"! Sounds like a good lyric for a hit song, doesn't it (laugh)?

Waiting for the Messiah

Neer: So Rabbi, in Kabbalah, who's the true Messiah?

Rabbi: You are (laugh).

Neer: Come on, I'm serious, when is the Messiah coming?

Rabbi: I'm serious too. He's already come and it's you. He's also me, and everybody else.

Neer: OK, you've lost me.

Rabbi: One of the primary teachings in Kabbalah is: always look within yourself—this is where all your questions will be answered. The Messiah isn't out there, he's in here.

Neer: In where?

Rabbi: Inside the essence of your being. Your Messiah is within you as a part of your Soul. IT'S a pure spark of the Godhead and IT wants to lead you to the Promised Land. But, first you must perform your own miracle.

Neer: ...and what's the miracle?

Rabbi: You must part the waters of your own Red Sea.

Neer: ...and how can I do that?

Rabbi: Remember in Exodus when God performs miracles through the rod of Moses?

Neer: You mean the rod that turned into a snake?

Rabbi: Yes, the snake that devoured Pharaoh's snakes.

Neer: I remember.

RABBI: Well, the snake or serpent is an ancient symbol of knowledge. When Moses' snake devoured Pharaoh's snakes, it was symbolic of the Hebrew's knowledge of monotheism devouring the old Egyptian knowledge of polytheism.

NEER: Now, that makes a lot of sense.

RABBI: ...and when Moses pointed the rod toward the Red Sea, a miracle occurred.

NEER: The Sea opened, and the Hebrews were able to cross-over into the desert.

RABBI: Yes, and so you must perform your own inner miracle.

NEER: ...and how can I do that?

RABBI: When you point the divine rod of your higher nature at the Red Sea of your lower nature, your Soul will be set free from bondage.

NEER: Ah-ha, I understand—and that's an excellent metaphor.

RABBI: ...and when your Soul reaches the other side of the shore, you'll wander through your own internal desert for awhile.

NEER: I hope I won't be wandering for forty years (laugh)?

RABBI: In your case, it may only take thirty-nine (laugh).

NEER: Speaking of forty, why is that particular number used so often in the Bible?

RABBI: Well, for starters, it's the numerical value of the Hebrew letter Mem, which symbolizes water.

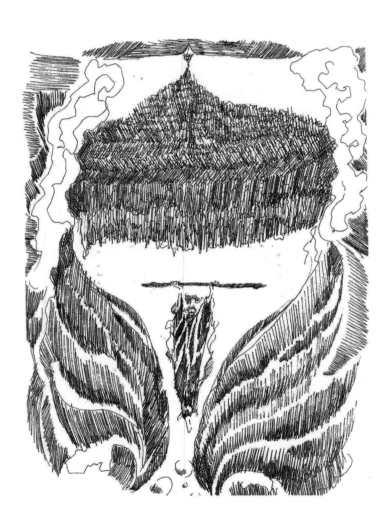

NEER: ...and why is water so important?

RABBI: It symbolizes cleansing and purification. Sometimes, we need a nice cold shower to wake us up.

NEER: I see.

RABBI: And since our bodies are composed of 60% water, it's an important mechanism for finding physical and mental balance.

NEER: ...and so, we wander through our own internal desert until we find balance in our lives?

RABBI: Yes, and balance is what we'll find in Tiphereth. We'll also find our own inner Messiah who's ready to transform us into a son or daughter of God at anytime.

NEER: ...and when does this transformation begin?

RABBI: Whenever you're ready. Just like the Hebrews who crossed over the River Jordan, the Soul will crossover the Sephira Yesod and arrive in the Promised Land of Tiphereth. Then, life truly becomes Heaven on Earth.

NEER: So, there's no reason to wait for a savior to rescue mankind?

RABBI: Why wait, when we can start right now? We can transform ourselves into divine beings anytime we want to. So, my suggestion is—everyone should get started as quickly as possible.

NEER: I agree.

RABBI: Then go to work!

NEER: (Smiling) I will.

RABBI: Good.

NEER: But, there's another "forty" I'm curious about. Wasn't there a rule among Kabbalists which said, "no one under forty" should study Kabbalah?

RABBI: There was such a rule a long time ago.

NEER: But, why forty again? Why not thirty, or fifty?

RABBI: The Rabbis thought that a man needed at least forty years of life experience before he could grasp the complexities of Kabbalah.

NEER: ...and today, you don't have to be forty, and you certainly don't have to be a man?

RABBI: That's right. Lately, I've seen more women studying Kabbalah than men. There's an ever increasing number of young people who are also excellent students. There are people of all faiths and ethnic backgrounds who have found answers to life's most difficult questions by learning Kabbalah. Most importantly, there are no rules, regulations or requirements about age, race, religion or nationality when studying these sacred universal truths. So, you see my friend, Kabbalah is truly for everyone!

WAITING FOR THE MESSIAH (WITHIN)

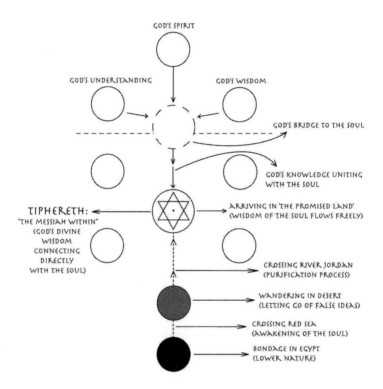

GOD'S SPIRIT

GOD'S UNDERSTANDING

GOD'S WISDOM

GOD'S BRIDGE TO THE SOUL

GOD'S KNOWLEDGE UNITING WITH THE SOUL

TIPHERETH:
"THE MESSIAH WITHIN"
(GOD'S DIVINE WISDOM CONNECTING DIRECTLY WITH THE SOUL)

ARRIVING IN 'THE PROMISED LAND' (WISDOM OF THE SOUL FLOWS FREELY)

CROSSING RIVER JORDAN (PURIFICATION PROCESS)

WANDERING IN DESERT (LETTING GO OF FALSE IDEAS)

CROSSING RED SEA (AWAKENING OF THE SOUL)

BONDAGE IN EGYPT (LOWER NATURE)

The Sacred Name of God

NEER: Rabbi, what is the sacred name of God?

RABBI: There are many, but in Kabbalah there are four Hebrew letters. They form the Tetragrammaton.

NEER: The what?

RABBI: Well, to make it simple, let's just say, "The Sacred Name."

NEER: Thank you.

RABBI: You're welcome. Now, the Sacred Name is composed of Y-H-V-H.

NEER: Is that Yahweh?

RABBI: Yes, but IT'S also pronounced Yahveh, Jehovah, and sometimes Adonai. But, there's more to it than that.

NEER: I had a feeling there was.

RABBI: The first letter Yod symbolizes the Father, the next letter Hé is the Mother, the Vau is the Son and the final Hé is the Bride.

NEER: ...and do these four letters correspond to the Four Worlds of Existence?

RABBI: Yes! You're catching on! The Y represents the first World of Atziluth, H is the second World of Briah, V is the third World of Yetzirah, and the final H is the fourth World of Assiah.

NEER: So, these four letters represent everything there is.

RABBI: "Everything There Is, That Was, and Shall Be."

THE TETRAGRAMMATON

יהוה

PRONOUNCED: 'YAVEH', 'YAWEH' OR 'JAHOVAH'
(SOMETIMES ADONAI)

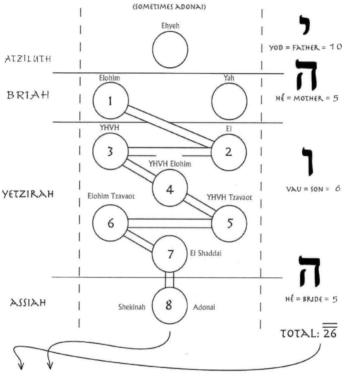

ATZILUTH

Ehyeh

YOD = FATHER = 10

BRIAH

Elohim — 1

Yah

HÉ = MOTHER = 5

YETZIRAH

YHVH — 3

El — 2

YHVH Elohim — 4

Elohim Tzavaot — 6

YHVH Tzavaot — 5

7 — El Shaddai

VAU = SON = 6

ASSIAH

Shekinah — 8 — Adonai

HÉ = BRIDE = 5

TOTAL: 26

2 + 6 = 8 ASPECTS OF GOD UNFOLD IN THE OLD TESTAMENT

8| VERTICALLY SYMBOLIZES THE FINITE UNIVERSE

∞ HORIZONTALLY SYMBOLIZES THE INFINITE NATURE OF THE GODHEAD

SPELLING OF THE WORD "TORAH" = TAV (400) + VAU (6) + RESH (200) + HÉ (5) = 611
611 ADDED AS SINGLE DIGITS: 6+1+1=8

TOTAL NUMBER OF WORDS IN THE TORAH = 79,856
ADDED AS SINGLE DIGITS: 7+9+8+5+6=35   3+5=8

That's why it's the Name of God.

NEER: ...and does each letter of the Sacred Name have a numerical value?

RABBI: Yes, let's take a look at how Gematria, or Kabbalistic numerology, uses mathematics to define the Sacred Name.

NEER: I'm ready.

RABBI: Good. Now, If we add up the numerical values of these four Hebrew letters: Yod (10) +Hé (5) +Vau (6) +Hé (5)—the total is 26. And, the middle pillar on the Tree of Life includes the following values: Keter (1) +Tiphereth (6) +Yesod (9) +Malkuth (10) =26. Then, we break this number down even further by adding 2+6 which equals 8. So, 8 is the important number here.

NEER: ...and why is that?

RABBI: Because, 8 symbolizes the Godhead in manifestation. When you turn 8 on its side, it's the symbol of Infinity ∞.

NEER: ...and God is infinite?

RABBI: Yes, and infinity is probably the best word to describe God.

NEER: So, how is the number 8 used in the Bible?

RABBI: There are 8 aspects of the Godhead mentioned in the Bible. First, God is introduced to us as Elohim in Genesis. From there IT descends in the following order: El, YHVH, YHVH-Elohim, YHVH-Tzabaoth, Elohim-Tzabaoth, El-Shaddai and Shekinah/Adonai.

NEER: So, 8 aspects of the Godhead descend toward the Earth?

RABBI: Yes, in language and in numbers.

NEER: ...and what are these numbers trying to tell us?

RABBI: The story of Creation, Progression and Decay. The Yod and the Hé represent the Father and the Mother. Together, they create the Vau who is their Son. The Son is our progressive Universe, and his Bride—the Shekinah or the final Hé—is our decaying planet Earth.

NEER: I understand. Now, you've mentioned the Shekinah before; can you tell me more about her?

RABBI: Yes, the word Shekinah is a feminine noun. Maimonides regarded the Shekinah as an intermediary between God and our World. Rabbi Nahmanides believed the Shekinah was the dwelling aspect of God. In the *Zohar*, the Shekinah is called, "the indwelling Feminine Presence" who is invited back by her Groom (the community of Israel) every Sabbath eve to sustain the world for another six days. Sometimes, she's referred to as "The God of Moses," because she protected the Hebrews after they escaped from Egypt. This feminine aspect of God is one of the most powerful images in Kabbalah.

NEER: My Mother will be happy to hear about her. She likes to empower herself over my Father whenever possible (laugh).

RABBI: (Laugh) Don't I know it! My wife belongs to that same club (laugh)! Ah yes....

NEER: I'm completely fascinated, please continue.

RABBI: OK, I was speaking about the letters of the Tetragrammaton.

NEER: You said, the Father "Y", and the Mother "H", create a Son "V". The Son marries the Shekinah, and they make spiritual progress together during a given life-cycle.

RABBI: That's right, keep going....

NEER: ...then, after the progressive phase is over, there comes a time of decay which lasts until the Universe comes to an end.

RABBI: Very good!

NEER: ...and then, there comes a time of rest when nothing happens, and there's only "Darkness upon the face of the Deep."

RABBI: That's right! And the next Universe will be waiting right around the corner.

NEER: Wow! I'm actually beginning to understand this stuff.

RABBI: You understand more than you know. Remember, it's all inside of you. It's all just waiting to be.....remembered (smile).

NEER: I hope so.

RABBI: I know so.

Good vs. Not-So-Good

NEER: Rabbi, some people say Kabbalah is dangerous because it conjures up evil spirits.

RABBI: Really? I've been told, "it's not the dead to be scared of—it's the living" (laugh).

NEER: Well, are there demons in Kabbalah?

RABBI: Yes, they're the ones teaching Kabbalah classes and charging big fees (laugh).

NEER: (Laugh) Can you please be serious?

RABBI: OK, you want demons? I'll give you demons. There are references to the Qlippoth in the *Zohar*.

NEER: ...and what are they?

RABBI: They are shells.

NEER: Shells of what?

RABBI: They are fragments of former physical embodiments which represent the human vices.

NEER: In other words, they're demons.

RABBI: Mythologically speaking—yes.

NEER: ...and what else can the Qlippoth refer to?

RABBI: Sometimes, they're called former worlds which didn't go according to plan. Noah lived in this type of world and God destroyed it by causing the great flood.

NEER: So, how can the demon-type of Qlippoth make spiritual progress and move forward?

RABBI: They must extinguish their vices.

NEER: ...and how does this transformation take place?

RABBI: Do you remember the story of Dr. Jekyll and Mr. Hyde?

NEER: ...with Spencer Tracy? I saw the movie a long time ago.

RABBI: Well, let me refresh your memory. The virtuous Dr. Jekyll invents a potion to rid humanity of its evils.

NEER: Sounds like a great idea.

RABBI: Yes, but when he tries the potion on himself, his own evil nature overpowers him.

NEER: So, the evil Mr. Hyde triumphed over the good Dr. Jekyll?

RABBI: That's right. The experiment failed, and evil triumphed over good.

NEER: That's not a very happy ending.

RABBI: There can't be a happy ending if we're foolish enough to believe that a magic potion will extinguish our personal demons.

NEER: So, I'll never have a little blue pill to purify my Soul?

RABBI: Highly unlikely. You'll have to do it all by yourself.

NEER: ...and, how will Kabbalah help me face my own demons?

RABBI: First, you must look into the mirror and take moral responsibility for everything you've ever thought, said and done. In other words, you must know who you are.

Neer: So, who am I?

Rabbi: You're a combination of an angel and a....nice Qlip-poth (smile).

Neer: A nice demon? (laugh)

Rabbi: Let's not use the word demon, OK? Let's stick with the term "lower nature."

Neer: OK, so, I'm living through my lower nature?

Rabbi: Yes, but don't feel bad, almost everyone on Earth is living this way.

Neer: So, how can I rid myself of my own lower nature?

Rabbi: By letting go of your false ideas and replacing them with Truth.

Neer: ...and Kabbalah can help me do this?

Rabbi: Yes. Let's take a look at the Tree of Life for a moment.

Neer: OK.

Rabbi: There's a constant ping-pong match going on between good and evil. This is symbolized on the Tree of Life by the interplay between Chesed (mercy and compassion) and Geburah (severity and judgment). One is on the left side of the Tree, the other is on the right. They represent Light and Darkness, or the Yin and Yang of the Sephirothal Tree. So, when Chesed and Geburah are properly balanced, Tiphereth will become radiant.

Neer: So, where do I find this "yellow brick road" that leads to Tiphereth?

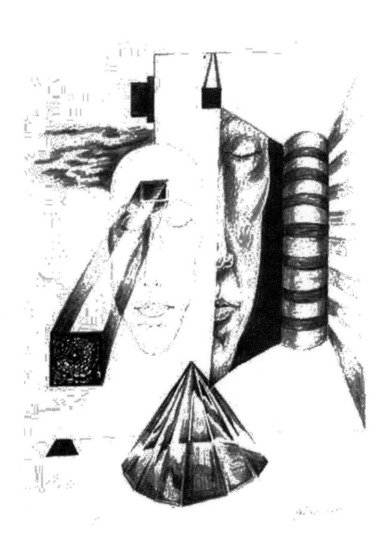

RABBI: First, you must acquaint yourself with your "higher nature."

NEER: ...and how can I do that?

RABBI: Just let your breath be silent and your thoughts be still. And from the depths of your silence listen to the Truth. Breathe in love and light; breathe out love to all the world. So try this my friend, and before you know it, your Sephira Tiphereth will be illuminating your Soul.

NEER: Rabbi, please define the word "Soul."

RABBI: In Kabbalah there are five aspects of the Soul, but let's concentrate on the Big Three.

NEER: OK.

RABBI: The first part is Neshamah—it's your pure spark of God. The second is Ruach—the seat of your spiritual judgment. The third part is Nephesh—your breath of life and instinctual nature.

NEER: ...and how do these three parts work together?

RABBI: Well, the third part, Nephesh works all by itself. It's the involuntary movements of the body. The heart beats, the blood circulates, hair grows and so forth.

NEER: ...and what about the other two?

RABBI: The second part is Ruach. It's defined by your judgments, desires, intentions, passions, thoughts, emotions and reason. From Ruach, you're constantly creating new causes which will have their effects later on.

NEER: Now, is cause and effect similar to "reaping what you sow"?

RABBI: Yes, but you can stop creating causes anytime you want. So, if you're only performing self-LESS acts of kindness and love, you'll never have to worry about suffering any adverse effects.

NEER: I like that idea. And you also mentioned Neshamah?

RABBI: Neshamah is your pure spark of God and ITS radiance fills you up with God's love. But sometimes, our

mental fog forms a dark shroud over the Soul, and the bright light of Neshamah can't shine through. This is when we slip into despair.

NEER: So, we must rid ourselves of this mental fog?

RABBI: Yes, because the fog is really our lower nature.

NEER: So, how do we overcome the strong desires of our lower nature?

RABBI: By allowing all three parts of the Soul to work together in harmony. Then, the divine light of Neshamah will shower you with God's love, wisdom, and understanding.

NEER: So, we must eliminate our lower nature so the white light of Neshamah can shine through us?

RABBI: You got it.

NEER: So, is my Neshamah shining right now?

RABBI: It's always ready to shine. But first, you must stop trying to acquire, possess, manipulate, force, and direct your life by controlling people, places and things.

NEER: So, I have a lot of work to do.

RABBI: Of course you do. We all do, and that's why we're here—and we're all in this together.

NEER: That's nice to know.

RABBI: ...and, you're moving in the right direction my friend. Just keep studying Kabbalah. It's the most profound "instruction manual" that has ever been written on how to live a good life.

NEER: ...and that's exactly what I plan on doing.

RABBI: Good, because when your Neshamah is fully illuminated, you will live your life for the sake of helping and teaching others.

NEER: ...and that sounds good to me.

RABBI: Trust me, Neer, when the bright light of Neshamah shines through you—you'll have no other choice but to give freely of yourself—and, I assure you, there's no better feeling in this world than being showered with the goodness, compassion and beauty of God's love!

ADAM WHO?

NEER: Rabbi, who is Adam Kadmon?

RABBI: I thought you might ask about him. He's not Adam of the Bible.

NEER: OK, then, who is he?

RABBI: He's "the Man" (laugh).

NEER: I'm a little confused.

RABBI: Good (laugh). When the Elohim say, "let us make man in our own image," they are speaking about Adam Kadmon. Adam means "humanity" and the Elohim create him as the human prototype of Man. Sometimes, like Elvis, he's called "the King."

NEER: So, why does he have a last name?

RABBI: Kadmon? It's like a title, it can be translated as, "the only Son of God."

NEER: Hmmm, that sounds a lot like the Christian phrase, "the only begotten Son."

RABBI: That's true. Many of the early Christians were Kabbalists, so there are many similarities. In the New Testament, Jesus is referred to as, "the second Adam." So, the gospel writers clearly understood Adam Kadmon's place in Kabbalah as the first-born Son of God.

NEER: So, there's overlapping symbolism in Judaism and Christianity?

RABBI: Of course. There was a Jewish group called the Essenes who broke away from traditional Judaism at the beginning of the first century CE. the Dead Sea Scrolls

ADAM KADMON

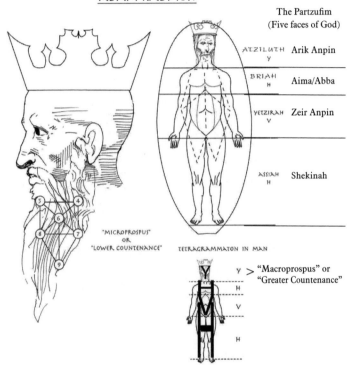

The Partzufim
(Five faces of God)

ATZILUTH
y — Arik Anpin

BRIAH
H — Aima/Abba

YETZIRAH
V — Zeir Anpin

ASSIAH
H — Shekinah

"MICROPROSPUS"
OR
"LOWER COUNTENANCE"

TETRAGRAMMATON IN MAN

y > "Macroprospus" or
"Greater Countenance"

H

V

H

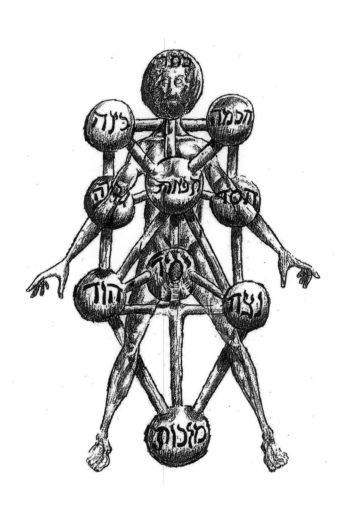

confirm this. The Essenes were Kabbalists and Jesus was the leader of this group. Many years later, this same group was known as the Gnostics, and eventually, the Christian Gnostics. In 325 CE, the New Testament was written and the word Gnostic was dropped entirely.

NEER: So, there are Kabbalistic influences in Christianity?

RABBI: Sure, it's only logical. The Essenes were Kabbalists, the Apostles were Kabbalists, and since the gospel writers were all familiar with Kabbalah, no other conclusion can be reached. Why else would the early Christians have kept the Old Testament with all its Kabbalistic references in their Bible?

NEER: I see what you mean.

RABBI: Religions are always evolving and changing. Just as Buddha was a Hindu who wanted to reform Hinduism, Jesus was a Jew who wanted to reform Judaism. Whenever any religion hits a snag, an agent of change comes along and tries to regenerate its original teachings.

NEER: But, don't some religions always stay the same?

RABBI: No, nothing ever stays the same. Eventually, everything changes. There is always a forward progression.

NEER: Can you give me an example?

RABBI: OK, remember, the Mercury Space Program of the 1950's?

NEER: I've seen it on the History Channel (laugh).

RABBI: Let's say Mercury was the Religion of Space Exploration at that time. So, using this analogy, Mercury evolved into the Gemini Program, which evolved into Apollo, which evolved into the Shuttle program and the Space Station. A hundred years from now, there will be far more advanced programs. My point is, if the Religion of Space is constantly evolving, so is the Religion of Man.

NEER: I understand, and since we're on the subject of Space, what does Kabbalah say about "the Big Bang" theory?

RABBI: Ah yes, Mr. Einstein used mathematics to prove what ancient philosophers had known for thousands of years. So, let's take a look at the birth of our Universe.

Rabbi: First, we must ask, what existed before "the Big Bang"?

Neer: OK.

Rabbi: We're talking about the most powerful explosion that could ever be created—it was a divine occurrence. So, the question is, what were the causes that led up to this explosion?

Neer: ...and Kabbalah has the answer?

Rabbi: Yes, and like everything else Kabbalah teaches, if we look within ourselves, we'll find the answer.

Neer: So, if I look within myself, I can figure out how the Universe was born?

Rabbi: Yes. Now, I want you to think about you and your Mother.

Neer: OK, I'm thinking about her, and she's probably worried.

Rabbi: Why?

Neer: I don't know; she's always worried.

Rabbi: Then, don't interfere with her worrying—but, you should call her tonight anyway.

Neer: OK, (smile) I will.

Rabbi: Good. Now think. Where were you, before you were born?

Neer: Inside my worried Mother.

AIN-SOPH USING ASPECTS OF ITSELF
TO CREATE THE UNIVERSE

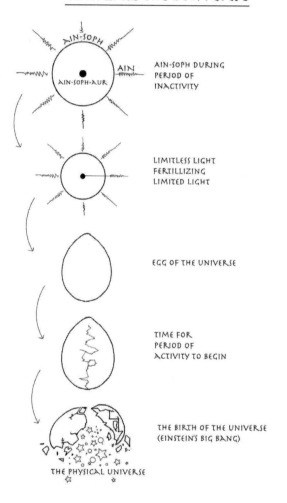

AIN-SOPH DURING
PERIOD OF
INACTIVITY

LIMITLESS LIGHT
FERTILLIZING
LIMITED LIGHT

EGG OF THE UNIVERSE

TIME FOR
PERIOD OF
ACTIVITY TO BEGIN

THE BIRTH OF THE UNIVERSE
(EINSTEIN'S BIG BANG)

THE PHYSICAL UNIVERSE

RABBI: Right, and before your birth you were resting in another world. Then, the hour struck and you experienced a powerful explosion. Then, all of a sudden, there was a "big bang" and whoosh—your life began in the physical world.

NEER: That's a very good analogy.

RABBI: Thank you. So, when you ask, what existed before the Universe? Try to imagine a cosmic embryo which was resting, growing and waiting for its birthday.

NEER: So, how does the Mother of the Universe become pregnant?

RABBI: Light impregnating light, or the symbolic immaculate conception.

NEER: So, that's where the story comes from? A virgin birth of light?

RABBI: Yes.

NEER: ...and when God says, "Let there be Light?"

RABBI: It's the same idea. Ain-Soph—the No-Thing, Without End—is symbolized by three aspects of light. The first part is outside the circle—it's called, Ain. The second part is the circle itself—Ain-Soph. The third is the dot inside the circle—Ain-Soph-Aur.

NEER: So, how does light fertilize itself?

RABBI: Ain is the prototype for male sperm. Ain-Soph is the prototype for the female egg. Ain-Soph-Aur is the nucleus of the female egg, just waiting to be fertilized by the light of Ain.

NEER: So, the human process of birth is modeled after cosmic birth?

RABBI: Yes! It's perfectly logical, isn't it?

NEER: I've never heard a better explanation.

RABBI: And these three aspects of light correspond to: the Father (Ain), the Mother (Ain-Soph) and the Son (Ain-Soph-Aur).

NEER: ...and how are these three aspects of light symbolized in the Sacred Name of God?

RABBI: Well, the first three letters of the Tetragrammaton are: Y, H and V—or the Father, the Mother and the Son.

NEER: ...and that sounds a lot like the Father, the Son and the Holy Spirit in Christianity.

RABBI: ...and that's because the Holy Trinity is based upon this specific Kabbalistic teaching. These Hebrew letters which form the Sacred Name of God are exactly the same in both religions.

NEER: So, there's a universal theme developing here?

RABBI: Yes, there are universal, intuitive truths which have been passed down throughout the ages. Understanding them is the key to understanding Kabbalah.

NEER: ...and that's what I'm trying to do, but some of this stuff is very difficult to follow.

RABBI: Of course it is. That's why in mythology, Kabbalah was given to the 70 elders, and the Torah was given to the 600,000.

NEER: Wow, that's only one-tenth of one percent!

RABBI: Really? I'm surprised the percentage was even that high (laugh).

The Sephirot In The Four Worlds

NEER: Rabbi, how are the Sephirot formed?

RABBI: I'm glad you asked. After Ain-Soph fertilizes IT-SELF, the process of differentiation begins, and the Godhead begins ITS descension from Atziluth, or the World of Thought, down to Assiah, or the World of Expression. As the process unfolds, the emanating Sephirot begin to form a Tree of Life in each of the Four Worlds.

NEER: So, there are really four Sephirothal Trees?

RABBI: Yes, one in each world. This is symbolized in the Bible by the four figures of Ezekiel's Chariot and the four faces on each figure.

NEER: ...and in each World does the life-wave begin at the top of the Tree and descend to the bottom?

RABBI: Yes. The first Sephira—Keter or the Godhead—sends down a massive shock-wave through the other nine Sephirot to form the Tree of Life. After the first Tree is formed, a second Tree starts to form in Briah – the less ethereal World below. Then, a third Tree begins to form on the astral plane of Yetzirah, and finally, we fall into matter in the Fourth World of Assiah.

NEER: So Rabbi, is all of humanity on the bottom sphere of the bottom Tree, at the bottom level of reality? Sounds like the bottom of the barrel to me.

RABBI: (Laugh) Not exactly rock-bottom. Don't forget, our life-energies have passed through the mineral, plant and animal kingdoms, so we've really made tremendous progress!

NEER: I think you're putting a positive spin on all this (laugh). And what happens after we've finished our work in the Human Kingdom?

RABBI: Oh gosh, you're really testing me today. I think I'll have another cookie before tackling that one, my friend (smile).

RABBI: So Neer, what happens after you've completed your human experience?

NEER: I thought I was asking the questions here (laugh).

RABBI: Well, now it's my turn—OK?

NEER: Sure, but I can only guess.

RABBI: That's good enough. I'm sure your guesses are better than most.

NEER: OK, I'm ready.

RABBI: So, what happens after the Soul is finished with life on Earth?

NEER: Well, maybe we become Angels.

RABBI: Good guess. Now, why is the Angelic Kingdom the next logical step along the way?

NEER: Ah...forward progression?

RABBI: You're a good guesser, my friend. And the first Biblical Angel appears to whom?

NEER: Ahhh...Abraham?

RABBI: Before Abraham.

NEER: I give up. I guess I've used up all my lucky guesses (laugh).

RABBI: OK, remember when mythical Adam and Eve were evicted from the Garden of Eden?

NEER: Yes.

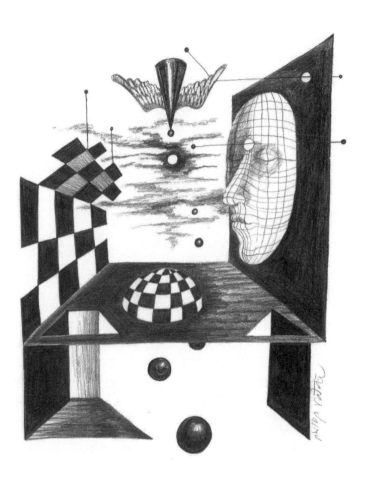

RABBI: Well, after they descended to Earth, God placed an Angel with a sword of fire at the bottom of the Tree of Life.

NEER: ...and this Angel blocked their way back to Eden, so they couldn't return to Paradise.

RABBI: Right, and from that time forward, Angels appear regularly in the Bible.

NEER: ...and who are the Archangels?

RABBI: Ah yes, they also play an important role in Kabbalah.

NEER: ...and what are their names?

RABBI: Michael, Raphael, Gabriel and Uriel, who is also known as Haniel.

NEER: ...and what exactly is an Archangel?

RABBI: Archangels are a combination of Jewish, Egyptian, Sumerian, Babylonian and Persian mythology. They are highly advanced spiritual beings who have great compassion for humanity, but they're never to be worshipped. We can use the Tree of Life in the World of Briah to specifically examine the Angelic Hierarchy.

NEER: Oh gosh, this sounds complicated, I better take notes.

RABBI: Good idea. Now, let's map out the location of the Archangels on the Tree of Life by matching them up with their corresponding Sephirot.

NEER: I'm ready.

RABBI: Then hold onto your seat. We find Raphael, "the healer" taking center-stage in Tiphereth, Uriel, "the giver of truth" is stage-right in Netzach, Michael, "who is like God" is stage-left in Hod, and Gabriel, "the communicator" is down-stage center in Yesod. Gabriel is the closest Archangel to the Earth plane, so that's why he interacts so often with mortals in the scriptures.

NEER:　...and what does an Archangel do?

RABBI:　Their primary mission is always the same. They help mankind whenever and however possible, but they don't interfere with the normal course of human events unless absolutely necessary.

NEER:　Can you give me an example?

RABBI:　Sure. Let's take a look at Archangel Gabriel. He makes his debut in the Book of Enoch sitting next to the Throne of God. Then, in the Old Testament, he saves Daniel in the lion's den. In the New Testament, he informs Mary she'll be giving birth to a Messiah, and 600 years later, he drops by to deliver the Koran to Mohammed.

NEER:　So, Gabriel gives equal time to all three religions?

RABBI:　Yes, just as Abraham is the Father of all three religions.

NEER:　So once again, there's a universal theme developing here?

RABBI:　Yes, and for Archangels like Gabriel, there were no religious boundaries.

NEER:　So, Angels have a universal love for all mankind?

RABBI:　Yes, and they are free of all prejudice and serve as non-denominational messengers of God.

NEER: I understand.

RABBI: Good.

NEER: Now, were Angels once human?

RABBI: Yes.

NEER: How do you know for sure?

RABBI: There are clues to follow, if you look for them.

NEER: Can you give me one?

RABBI: Sure, let's talk about the Peace Corps.

NEER: All right.

RABBI: Why do Peace Corps volunteers devote their time to helping those less fortunate?

NEER: They want to help humanity.

RABBI: ...and what's the benefit to them?

NEER: Just the experience of helping others.

RABBI: So, Peace Corps volunteers and Angels have something in common?

NEER: Yes, they both have good intentions and want to help others.

RABBI: Right, and they don't expect anything in return.

NEER: So, we're all Angels-in-training?

RABBI: Yes, we're all learning to become Angels by the self-LESS actions we perform.

NEER: So, I better sign up for the Peace Corps if I want to become an Angel!

RABBI: (Laugh) No, that wouldn't work. You must follow your own authentic path before ascending the Spiritual Ladder. Believe me, Neer, there are countless other ways you can be of service to mankind.

NEER: I understand.

RABBI: And, one day the entire Human Kingdom in Assiah will progress to the Angelic Kingdom in Yetzirah.

NEER: ...and the current Angelic Kingdom in Yetzirah will progress to the Archangelic World in Briah?

RABBI: (Smile) You're catching on, my friend.

NEER: ...and, this Angelic progression is symbolized by the ascending rungs on Jacob's Ladder?

RABBI: Precisely!

NEER: Now, how does the physical body also progress?

RABBI: Our bodies become lighter and more ethereal as we advance spiritually.

NEER: ...and the lighter we are, the closer we are to God?

RABBI: Yes indeed, and as we evolve spiritually, our Neshamah will bring us closer to God.

NEER: I understand, but when do we finally return to God?

RABBI: When the Soul is purified, it will become One with God.

NEER: ...and how long will that take?

RABBI: That's up to you. This isn't a bus station where they hand-out time schedules (laugh). After you've experienced all Four Worlds of the Spiritual Hierarchy, you'll be sent home once again.

NEER:　But, that could take an eternity!

RABBI:　Trust me, my friend, there's no rush. When you're living in Eternal Duration, time is irrelevant. As you allow the divine process to unfold, you'll always be right where you are at precisely the right moment. As King Solomon said:

> The race is not won by the swift,
> Nor the battle by the valiant,
> Nor is bread won by the wise,
> Nor wealth by the intelligent,
> Nor favor by the learned.
> Go eat your bread in gladness,
> And drink your wine in joy;
> For your action was long ago approved by God.
> Whatever it is within your power to do,
> Do it with all your might.

DEVEKUT: CLEAVING TO GOD

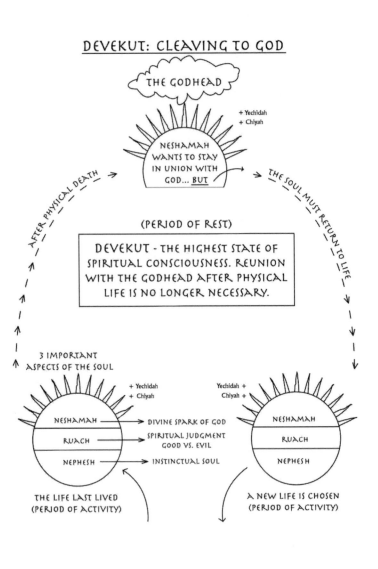

THE GODHEAD

+ Yechidah
+ Chiyah

NESHAMAH WANTS TO STAY IN UNION WITH GOD... BUT

AFTER PHYSICAL DEATH →

→ THE SOUL MUST RETURN TO LIFE

(PERIOD OF REST)

DEVEKUT - THE HIGHEST STATE OF SPIRITUAL CONSCIOUSNESS. REUNION WITH THE GODHEAD AFTER PHYSICAL LIFE IS NO LONGER NECESSARY.

3 IMPORTANT ASPECTS OF THE SOUL

+ Yechidah
+ Chiyah

NESHAMAH ——→ DIVINE SPARK OF GOD

RUACH ——→ SPIRITUAL JUDGMENT GOOD VS. EVIL

NEPHESH ——→ INSTINCTUAL SOUL

THE LIFE LAST LIVED (PERIOD OF ACTIVITY)

Yechidah +
Chiyah +

NESHAMAH

RUACH

NEPHESH

A NEW LIFE IS CHOSEN (PERIOD OF ACTIVITY)

What Happens After Death?

NEER: Rabbi, most people want to know what happens after they die.

RABBI: Oh, that's an easy one. Haven't you heard? They go to…Disney World (laugh).

NEER: (Laugh) That's good to know, please, sign me up (smile).

RABBI: You really want to know? Well, let's use the analogy of death and sleep.

NEER: OK.

RABBI: After the day is over, we go to sleep and dream, right?

NEER: Yes.

RABBI: Well, after every lifetime is over, your Soul goes to sleep and dreams too.

NEER: What does it dream about?

RABBI: The events of your prior lifetime.

NEER: …and what's the point of that?

RABBI: The Soul reviews the life last lived and takes an objective look at the lessons it has learned. It also takes time to reflect on where it's been and where it's going.

NEER: OK, and where does it go from there?

RABBI: The Soul always wants to stay with God, but it must go back to Earth and continue its journey.

NEER: ...and what if my Soul refuses to go back?

RABBI: It won't refuse—just like you didn't refuse to obey your parents when you were 5 years old.

NEER: So, my Soul must return to Earth?

RABBI: It may go reluctantly, but it will go back. It's all part of the Divine Plan.

NEER: But, isn't there one, last, final lifetime?

RABBI: Yes, and after it's over, your Soul will experience a state of consciousness called, Devekut—or "cleaving to God."

NEER: ...and how long does Devekut last?

RABBI: Ah...in your case, about 4 minutes (laugh).

NEER: Oh come on! (laugh).

RABBI: As long as it needs to. Devekut is a temporary state of bliss. It's like a beautiful dream which you hope will never end. But, the dream eventually comes to an end and the Soul wakes up.

NEER: ...and then what happens?

RABBI: The Soul returns to Earth and picks up right where it left off.

NEER: So, looking at the big picture, does the Soul continue to climb the ladder of the Spiritual Hierarchy?

RABBI: Yes it does. Our friend Enoch wrote about his experiences at higher levels of existence. He saw hundreds of thousands of enlightened beings serving God throughout the Universe. He said, "and I saw there was a very great light, and fiery troops of Archangels, Incorporeal forces and Dominions, Orders and Governments."

NEER: Oh no; there are governments up there too?

RABBI: Yes, but don't worry—from what I've heard, there aren't any political parties to mess things up (laugh)!

Golem or Tzaddik? Your Choice

RABBI: You haven't asked me about the legend of the Golem.

NEER: Isn't he a robot made out of clay?

RABBI: (Laugh) Well, sort of. As the story goes, he was created by man to act as his servant and protector.

NEER: Sounds like man was trying to play God?

RABBI: Yes, but the difference is, God created man with a Soul and man can't possibly compete with that.

NEER: Well, wait a minute, what about human cloning?

RABBI: That's different. Cloning is the duplication of an existing genetic blueprint; it's not the creation of the actual blueprint itself.

NEER: Good point. So, the Golem wasn't able to acquire a Soul?

RABBI: That's right, and after awhile he became frustrated because he wanted to become a real man.

NEER: So, how does this story relate to Kabbalah?

RABBI: Well, the Golem is a symbol of soul-less people in search of their own divinity.

NEER: ...and how do they find their divinity?

RABBI: Redemption.

NEER: ...and how does that happen?

RABBI: By understanding the wisdom of Kabbalah and becoming a Tzaddik.

NEER: A what?

RABBI: A "righteous one" who lives a virtuous life and performs Mitzvot for all mankind.

NEER: ...and Mitzvot are good deeds filled with kindness, love and compassion?

RABBI: That's right, and a Tzaddik performs Mitzvot all the time. When your actions are of pure intent, the effects of your actions can only be kind, loving and honorable.

NEER: So, what's the first step toward becoming a Tzaddik?

RABBI: When everything that was once important to you— becomes unimportant—you'll know you're on your way to becoming a Tzaddik.

NEER: So, if winning the lottery is important to me—is that wrong?

RABBI: There's no right or wrong here, my friend. This is not about money, cars, houses or jewelry. All these things should be enjoyed and you should live in style and comfort. However, if you win the lottery tomorrow, and then you lose it all in the stock market next week, how are you going to feel then?

NEER: Extremely depressed. I get depressed if I lose a hundred dollars at the blackjack table.

RABBI: ...and that's my point! Nothing outside of yourself should ever have the power to affect your state of mind. When your happiness is at the mercy of outside events, it can turn into misery at a moments notice.

NEER: But, can't material possessions also bring great joy?

The Golem

RABBI: Sure they can, but unless your inner core is intact, your experience of joy will always be temporary and conditional.

NEER: So, true, lasting happiness can only be found within myself?

RABBI: Yes, and that's Rule #1!

NEER: So, Kabbalah can help me find my own inner happiness?

RABBI: Yes, but that's the end-game—Kabbalah all by itself is not the solution. It's the assimilation of Kabbalistic teachings into the "who you are" which makes all the difference.

NEER: So, as I study Kabbalah, when should I expect to see some results?

RABBI: I don't know. This isn't a weight-loss program where you'll see results in the first two weeks (laugh). This is the work of a lifetime. Your spiritual advancement strictly depends upon your own determination, perseverance and devotion.

NEER: So, I can progress at my own pace, and I'm only accountable to myself when studying Kabbalah?

RABBI: Correct. There's no one testing you, grading you or judging you—other than—you. Just learn at your own pace and take as much time as you need. There's no hurry and there's no race to be won.

NEER: I feel very comfortable with that approach.

RABBI: Good, then your life will definitely change for the better—there's not a single doubt in my mind!

NEER: ...well, if you have no doubts, then I'll dismiss all doubts, too (smile).

RABBI: Trust me my friend, you never want to be a Golem— you always want to be a Tzaddik! And when you are, your life will always be filled with three things: love, wisdom and joy!

NEER: ...and all I can say to that is: Amen (smile).

Lost Books of the Bible

NEER: Rabbi, please tell me more about the Book of Enoch?

RABBI: What would you like to know?

NEER: Why isn't it in the Bible?

RABBI: It was nearly 2,000 years ago. When they found the Dead Sea Scrolls, they also found ancient Bibles and the Book of Enoch was included with the book of The Prophets.

NEER: So, there really are "lost books" of the Bible?

RABBI: Of course, and Kabbalah has been the vehicle for passing along their timeless messages.

NEER: So, the essence of these lost books was never really lost?

RABBI: That's right, because Truth can never be lost. It's only mankind who gets lost every once in awhile.

NEER: ...but, in spite of it all, mankind is still moving forward, right?

RABBI: That's right, and I want YOU to keep moving forward by studying and absorbing the ancient wisdom of Kabbalah.

NEER: I certainly will, Rabbi.

RABBI: I know you will (yawn)...and now my friend, I must start moving forward myself. You've kept me up way past my bedtime (smile), but it's all right—I'll forgive you (smile).

NEER: (Smile) Thank you.

LOST BOOKS OF THE BIBLE

DEAD SEA SCROLLS AND ANCIENT BIBLES DISCOVERED IN 1947

THESE LOST BOOKS OF THE BIBLE FORM
PART OF THE SACRED LITERATURE OF THE
ALEXANDRIAN JEWS CIRCA 50 AD - 100 AD
(ACCORDING TO HISTORIANS PHILO AND JOSEPHUS).

BOOKS WRITTEN DURING
THE BABYLONIAN CAPTIVITY:

APOCRYPHA

LOST CHAPTERS OF
THE OLD TESTAMENT:

- TOBIT
- JUDITH
- THE REST OF ESTHER
- THE WISDOM OF SOLOMON
- ECCLESIASTICUS
- BARUCH WITH THE EPISTLE OF JEREMIAH
- THE SONG OF THE THREE HOLY CHILDREN
- THE HISTORY OF SUZANNA
- BEL AND THE DRAGON
- I MACCABEES
- II MACCABEES

- JUBILEES
- I ENOCH
- BEN SIRA (SIRACH)
- THE EPISTLE OF JEREMIAH
- TOBIT

Enoch walking with God.

RABBI: ...and who knows? Maybe one day you'll write a book about this intriguing conversation we've just had (laugh).

NEER: Maybe I will.

RABBI: I hope you do, but please don't write about all the cookies I've eaten today.

NEER: Don't worry—that will be our little secret. Rabbi, I can't thank you enough for sharing your lifetime's worth of knowledge, understanding and experience with me today! You've truly enlightened my Spirit and enlivened my Soul!

RABBI: Neer, my good friend, it has been my absolute pleasure. We've shared a rare and exceptional moment together. And, as Bogart said in *Casablanca,* "I think this could be the beginning of a beautiful friendship." But, in the meantime—until we meet again—may God bless you and keep you!

Epilogue

The book you have just read has been purposely structured as a curriculum guide for introducing the new student to Kabbalah. The most important Kabbalistic frameworks have been explained and the main topics have been discussed. Now, it's up to you to delve deeper into the specific areas of study which appeal to you. Eventually, you will find all paths leading to one central point in Kabbalistic philosophy. So, take your time, meditate on these sacred teachings, and soon you will see many positive changes taking place in your life.

After my life-changing encounter with Rabbi Abraham, I was anxious to read as many books on Kabbalah as possible. I scoured libraries, bookstores and the internet frantically seeking additional information about all the topics I had discussed with the Rabbi. After reading dozens of books by mainstream and little-known Kabbalists, I have found Gershom Scholem to be the most authoritative author on this subject. Scholem is widely recognized as the foremost Kabbalistic scholar of the 20th Century, and he provokes ongoing thought about the deepest questions concerning the nature of mysticism. He spent most of his life dispelling the many myths and exaggerations about the history of Kabbalah, and he proves his claims through dialect, syntax and analysis of ancient documents.

I am sad to report that my good friend and teacher, Rabbi Abraham, passed on in 1998 at the blessed age of 96. He is still my guiding light and daily inspiration as I continue to learn more about this sacred and timeless philosophy. In our last conversation, when I hit a snag and was very confused, Rabbi Abraham said to me, "Remember Neer, pure Truth is like a blue diamond—it's buried deep down below the surface!" So, off I went—deep down within myself—and eventually, after searching, struggling and sifting through my own mental resistance—I finally found that elusive blue diamond of Truth.

—Bob Waxman
(Neer Aish-Donag)

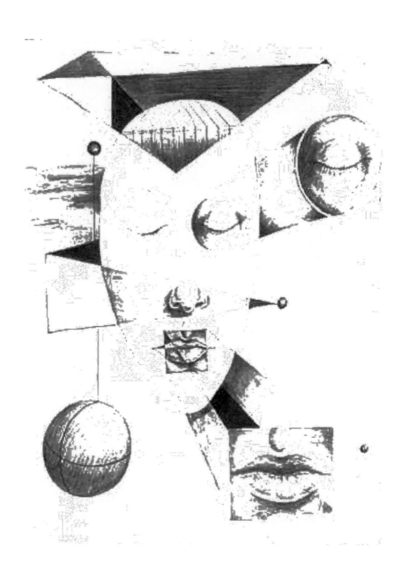

Kabbalistic Glossary of Commonly Used Words & Phrases

A

Abba-Amona—Father-Mother; esoteric names of the Sephirot Chokmah and Binah.

Abram—Abraham's original name in the Old Testament.

Abraham—son of Terah, husband of Sarah and Father of Isaac and Ishmael.

Adam—first man of the flesh in the Bible; translated as humanity, blood and red earth.

Adam Kadmon—the image or prototype of man in the Universe before Adam of the dust; the Heavenly King.

Adonai—commonly translated as, "the Lord"; sometimes substituted for Yahweh.

Aima—the Supernal Mother; associated with Binah.

Ain—the first veil of negative existence; the "No-thing" beyond human comprehension.

Ain-Soph, En-Sof, Eyn-Suph etc.—the second Veil of Negative Existence; "Without End," Infinite and unthinkable; "Everything That Is, That Was and Shall Be."

Ain-Soph-Aur—the third Veil of Negative Existence; "Limitless or Boundless Light"; the potential of all things yet to come.

Aries—symbolized by the ram; associated with the Hebrew letter Hé; the 15th Path on the Tree of Life.

Amen—so be it!; truth.

Anak—a giant.

Angels—spiritual beings with unique qualities; they live in the

World of Yetzirah.

Anpin—face or countenance.

Ararita—a name of God; one principle of his unity.

Aretz—Earth.

Arik Anpin—the Greater Countenance or Macroprospus; associated with the Sephira Keter.

Ashshaph—astrologer; magician.

Assiah—the fourth and lowest of the Four Kabbalistic Worlds, the World of Expression; the physical or material world associated with Malkuth; the final Hé in the Tetragrammaton.

Atziluth—The highest of the Four Kabbalistic Worlds, the World of Emanation; the divine prototype for the three Worlds below; associated with Keter; symbolized by the Yod in the Tetragrammaton.

Aur—light.

Avir—ethereal substance; associated with Briah.

B

Baal Shem—"Master of the Name"; Jewish magician.

Bahir—light or shining; the book *Bahir* is known as the *Book Of Light*.

Bar—son; pure; empty.

Belial—"without God"; opposite of Ain-Soph.

Beni Elohim—"Sons of God."

Bereshith—the first word in Genesis, "In the beginning."

Betulah—a virgin; associated with the tenth Sephira Malkuth.

Binah—"Understanding"; the third Sephira; associated with Hé of the Tetragrammaton.

Boaz—the black pillar at Solomon's Temple; symbolizes the feminine principle.

Bohu—void or emptiness.

Briah—the Second Kabbalistic World, the World of Creation; associated with the highest Archangels; the first Hé in the Tetragrammaton.

Bride—the 10th Sephira Malkuth; the Shekinah; the final Hé of the Tetragrammaton.

C

Cabala—the Christian interpretation of the ancient wisdom teachings.

Chai—life; living.

Chariot—the Merkabah as described in the Book of Ezekiel.

Chayim—life.

Cherubim—a high level of Angelic Beings associated with Chokmah.

Chesed—"Love or Mercy"; the fourth Sephira.

Chiah—an immortal part of the soul; the essence of Life; free will and the impulse to progress spiritually; associated with the Sephira Chokmah.

Chiim—a plural noun; 'lives' as in Elohim Chiim, 'the Gods of lives'.

Chitanuth-our—coats of skin given to Adam and Eve after the Fall.

Chokmah—"Wisdom"; the second Sephira; associated with the first Hé of the Tetragrammaton.

D

Daath—knowledge; the Abyss on the Tree of Life between Chokmah, Binah and Chesed, usually represented by a dotted circle.

Dabar—'The Word' or Plato's First Logos; a reflection of Ain-Soph.

Dagon—fish or Messiah.

Dibbuk—an evil spirit.

Din—"Justice"; another name for the 5th Sephira, Geburah.

Dinur—the "River of Fire" whose flame burns the Souls of the guilty in Kabbalistic mythology.

Double Image—the dual ego; the higher Metatron (man's Guardian Angel) and the lower Samael (man's Evil Demon).

Dudaim—the Soul and Spirit; any two things united in love and friendship; "happy is he who preserves his dudaim inseparable"; mandrakes, the plant was related to love charms and magic.

Dumah—the Angel of Silence or Death.

Dyookna—the shadow of eternal light; the "Angels of the Presence" or Archangels.

E

Echath—one; unity (feminine).

Echad—one; unity (masculine).

Eden—delight or pleasure; the Garden of Delight; a place for Initiation into the hidden Mysteries.

Edom—a deeply concealed mystery in the allegory of the Seven Kings of Edom; a kingdom of unbalanced forces and unstable character.

Eheieh/Ehyeh—"I AM"; name of the Godhead; associated with the Sephira Keter.

El—a divine name of God associated with Chesed.

Elohim—pluralilzed name of God associated with Binah; name of God in the first sentence of the Bible.

El Shaddai—"God Almighty"; a name of God associated with Yesod; the God of Jacob.

Elyonim—"Those who dwell above"; inhabitants of the three higher worlds on the Tree of Life.

Em—"Mother."

Emeth—truth; according to Kabbalistic mythology, it was written on the head of the Golem.

Enoch—son of Jared, father of Methuselah and great-grandfather of Noah; he was guided through the Seven Heavens by two Angels. He speaks with God and "walks with God" (*Book of Enoch*).

En-Sof—see Ain-Soph.

Eshmim—the Firmament which includes the Sun, planets and stars.

Essenes—a mysterious sect of Jews who lived near the Dead Sea in ancient times.

Etz ha-Chayim—"The Tree of Life"; Sephirothal Tree described in the *Sepher Yetzirah*.

Eve—first woman of the flesh in the Bible.

Ezekiel—one of the three major prophets; he wrote about the mysterious Merkabah in the Old Testament.

Ezra—a Jewish priest and scribe who compiled the *Pentateuch* and most of the Old Testament (circa 450 BCE).

F

Flaming Sword—the image of a lightening bolt creating the Tree of Life as it descends from Keter to Malkuth; the Godhead unfolding from Spirit into matter.

Four Worlds of Existence: Atziluth—Emanation, Briah—Creation, Yetzirah—Formation, Assiah—Expression. The essence of Ain-Soph concentrates ITSELF into the ten Sephirot in Atziluth and their reflections are produced in succession on each of the four lower planes; as Spirit descends into matter, there is a gradual lessening of radiance and purity until the material Universe comes into being.

G

Gabriel—"the Strength of God"; an Archangel associated with Sephira Yesod.

Gaihinnom/Gehenna—Hell in the Talmud.

Gaon—a great scholar or genius.

Gebor (Gebborim pl.); the most powerful Angels in Heaven; mighty men or giants mentioned in Genesis.

Geburah (Gevurah or Din)—"Judgment and Severity"; the fifth Sephira.

Gedulah—"Greatness or Magnificence"; associated with Sephira Chesed.

Gemara—Rabbinical commentary on the *Mishnah*.

Gematria—numerical values of Hebrew words determined by totaling the values of the letters in each word; one of the methods for extracting the hidden meanings of letters, words and sentences in Kabbalistic study.

Gilgul—cycles of rebirth and transformation of the Soul; the "whirling of the Soul" after death.

Golem—a legendary being of clay created by man to be his servant and protector.

Guff/Gof/Guph—body or physical form.

H

Habal de Garmin—spiritual body or image of the deceased; the inner fundamental spiritual form after death.

Hachoser—reflected lights; minor or inferior powers.

Haggadah—parts of the Talmud which are legendary.

Haima—the golden egg.

Hajaschar—creative forces or "Powers of Light".

Halakah (Halakhah)—"rule or law"; parts of the Talmud arguing various points of the doctrine.

Haniel—see Uriel.

Ha-Shem—the Ineffable Name; the Tetragrammaton.

Hattaah—sin.

Hé—fifth letter of the Hebrew alphabet; second and fourth letters of the Tetragrammaton, symbolizes the Mother and the Bride respectively; associated with the Worlds of Briah and Assiah; symbol of Aries; 15th Path on the Tree of Life.

Hayo-Bischat—the Devil or Tempter in the *Zohar*.

Hay-yoth-ha-Qadosh—the holy living creatures of Ezekiel's Merkabah or Chariot.

Hillel—a great Babylonian Rabbi, circa 100 BCE; founder of the Pharisees sect.

Hoa—That, from which proceeds Ab, "the Father."

Hod—"Splendor and Glory"; the eighth Sephira; a female passive potency.

I

Ibbur—a being possessed or occupied by the soul of a saintly individual.

Idra Raaba Qadisha—"The Greater Holy Assembly," one of the books of the *Zohar.*

Idra Zuta Qadisha—"The Lesser Holy Assembly," one of the books of the *Zohar.*

Ineffable Name—Eheieh, "I Am", sometimes, the name "Adonai" is substituted.

Isarim—the Initiates of the Essenes.

Israel—"he who strives with God"; name given to Jacob after he wrestled with an Angel in the desert. Sometimes translated as, "he who struggles with God."

J

Jachin—"to establish"; symbolic name for the white pillar at Solomon's Temple; corresponds to the masculine principle.

Jamin—the right side of man which is considered the most worthy; Benjamin, "son of the right side."

Jerusalem—"City of Peace."

K

Kabbalah/Kabala/Kabalah—from the Hebrew root-word KBL, "oral tradition" or "to receive"; often used as a generic term for Jewish mysticism.

Kabbalist/Kabalist—one who interprets the hidden meanings of the Scriptures.

Kabod (The)—a symbolic image of Atziluth represented by a great and radiant human figure. This Divine Man appears in the vision of the prophet Ezekiel who saw the Four Worlds. He sees the Presence Of God in Atziluth, the heavenly Throne in Briah, the Chariot in Yetzirah and the Wheels above the Earth in Assiah; the equivalent of Adam Kadmon.

Kalah—"Bride"; associated with Sephira Malkuth and the Shekinah.

Kav—the beam of Divine Will which fills the ten Sephirot of the Tree of Life.

Kavvanah – mystical meditation.

Kelippoth – see Qlippoth.

Keneset Yisrael—the community of Israel which is one with the Shekinah or Bride.

Kerubim—Angels associated with Sephira Yesod; associated with the Moon.

Keter—"Crown"; highest of the ten Sephirot; the Godhead; Macroprospus; the Vast Countenance.

Kings of Edom—Kings who reigned before "there were Kings in Israel"; early, malformed races of men; worlds that "failed" due to imbalances of Mercy and Severity.

Kohen—"priest".

Kol—"a voice"; the Voice of the Divine.

Kuch-ha-guf—"force"; electrical or astral body of man.

L

Lavanah—the Moon as a sacred planet and astral influence.

Leviathan—mythological sea monster.

Lilith—a female demon and first wife of Adam before Eve was created.

Lilin—the children of Lilith and their descendants.

Lower Face—the Lower Countenance or Microprospus.

M

Magen David—Star of David; six pointed star; also known as the "Seal of Solomon".

Maggid—teacher; inner guide; guardian angel.

Mahaseh Bereshith—the "Work of Creation"; Kabbalistic cosmology.

Malkah- "Queen"; associated with Sephira Malkuth.

Malachim (Malakim)—Angels or messengers.

Malkuth—the "Kingdom" or Earth; the tenth Sephira; the Bride or Shekinah.

Masorah/Melchites—the collection of notes, explanations, grammatical comments and critical commentaries found in the margins of ancient Hebrew scrolls.

Masoretic Points (vowels)—supposed to give the true pronunciation of Hebrew words by addition of points representing vowels to the consonants.

Matrona—identical to Malkuth or the "inferior Mother".

Mayim (Maim)—"water"; the ethereal substance preceding matter in the Creation of the Universe.

M'bul—"waters of the flood"; periodical crimes or iniquities of morality which cause earthly cataclysms.

Melech (Melekh)—"King"; associated with the Sephira Tiphereth; symbolized by the Vau of the Tetragrammaton.

Mekubbal—kabbalist; mystic.

Memrab—"the voice of the will"; the collective forces of Nature in activity.

Meracha-phath—"breathing" of the Divine Spirit while hovering over the waters of space before the Creation.

Merkabah—"Chariot"; Ezekiel's vision of a vehicle above the Earth carrying the Presence of God, the Throne, Angels and Wheels.

Messianic Awareness—the "Messiah Within"; dominant mindset of Tiphereth.

Metatron—"Prince of Faces"; intelligence of the Sephira Keter; in Gematria, his number is 314, the same as El Shaddai (the God of Jacob).

Metempsychoses—the progress of the Soul from one stage of existence to another; "a stone becomes a plant, a plant an animal, an animal a man, a man becomes a spirit and a spirit a God".

Michael—"Who is like God?"; Archangel associated with Sephira Hod.

Midrashim—"ancient"; post-Biblical Jewish writings; stories that teach and define the Law through dialogues between teacher and student.

Mishnah—the older portion of the Talmud, or "oral tradition," consisting of supplementary regulations and commentary for guidance of the Jews. It is used to understand the written transmission of the Torah; post-Biblical compilation of Jewish Law was completed circa 200 CE.

Mitzraim—translated as "Egypt" in the Old Testament; a "narrow place"; the point of departure for Moses and the Israelites after being freed from bondage.

Mitzvot (Mitzvah sing.)—a divine commandment or "binding point" to God; a good deed.

Moshiach—"the anointed one"; the Messiah who is to descend from the House of David.

Mount Moriah—site of Solomon's Temple; Abraham took Isaac there as a sacrifice to God (an Angel of God stopped him from killing his son).

N

Nabia—looking into the future using clairvoyant powers.

Nachash—"The Deprived" or "Magician"; serpent in Genesis; the power to imprison and to set free.

Nazar—those who are "set apart"; a monastic group mentioned in the Old Testament.

Nehashim—"The Serpent's works" or "the great deceiving Serpent"; ethereal light.

Nephesh—breath of Life; aspect of the Soul corresponding to natural instinct; the involuntary processes of the body.

Nephilim—giants or titans mentioned in Genesis.

Neshamah—divine spark of God; aspect of the Soul corresponding to pure Spirit; it is divided into three parts: 1) Yechidah—associated with Keter, the essence of Spirit or God, 2) Chiah—associated with Chokmah, the essence of Soul or Wisdom, and 3) Neshamah—associated with Binah, the essence of Intelligence or Mind.

Netzach—"Victory"; the seventh Sephira corresponding to human emotions; a masculine potency.

Noahide Laws—Seven Divine Laws given by God to Noah for all humanity to obey.

Notarikon (Notariqon)—formation and interpretation of words from Hebrew initials or "finals" in every sentence; formation of acronyms; each letter of a word represents an entirely new word; breaking down a long word into two smaller words which have meanings of their own.

Nukva—the bride of the Microprosopus or the Presence of the Shekinah. The Shekinah is held captive by the Qlippoth which surround Malkuth. She is either freed or kept in bondage by the physical activities initiated by Zeir Anpin (the Lesser Countenance).

O

Ob (Sprit of)—a person who used the ethereal light to contact Spirits.

Odem (ADM)—a red stone on the breast-plate of a high Jewish Priest.

Onech—the bird Phoenix named after Enoch; Initiator and Instructor.

Otz (Etz) Chiim—The Tree of Life with its ten Sephirot and three columns.

Oulam—a period of time with an unknown beginning and end.

Oz—strength; violence; glory.

P

Partzufim—"Visages"; faces; personal aspects of Adam Kadmon.

Paschad—fear; associated with Sephira Geburah.

Pashut—"literal interpretation"; one of the four ways of interpreting the *Bible*.

Philo Judaeus—famous Jewish historian and writer, born circa 30 BCE, died circa 45 CE. His works contain metaphysical theories, high ethical standards and esoteric teachings.

Q

Qabalah—Hermetic interpretation of the ancient wisdom teachings.

Qlippoth (Kelippoth)—"Shells" of prior worlds or shells of physical bodies; the lower world of darkness and demons such as Samael and Lilith.

R

Rabbi Abulafia—born 1240 CE, formed a Kabbalistic school named after him. His most famous writings are the *Seven Paths of Law* and the *Epistle to Rabbi Solomon*.

Rabbi Akiba—author of a famous Kabbalistic work, the *Alphabet of R.A.* Every letter is a symbol of an esoteric idea.

Rabbi Azriel ben Menachem (1160 CE)—author on the *Commentary on the Ten Sephirot*. He was a pupil of Isaac the Blind and the teacher of Rabbi Moses Nachmonides.

Rabbi Gikatilla (1300 CE)—a distinguished Kabbalist who wrote,

The Garden of Nuts, The Gate to the Vowel Points, The Mystery of the Shining Metal and *The Gates of Righteousness.* He stressed the importance of Gematria, Notarikon and Temura.

Rabbi Isaac the Blind (1200 CE)—the first Rabbi who taught Kabbalah in Europe.

Rabbi Luria—founded a school of Kabbalah, circa 1560.

Rabbi Moses Cordovero (1550 CE)—author of such widely respected Kabbalistic books as, *The Garden of Pomegranates, A Sweet Light* and *The Book of Retirement;* noted for his adherence to metaphysical teachings.

Rabbi Moses de Leon (circa 1200 CE)—according the world's foremost Kabbalistic scholars, he was the author, editor and publisher of the *Zohar.*

Rabbi Moses Maimonides (circa 1150 CE)—famous Rabbi and author of the great work, *The Guide for the Perplexed.*

Rabbi Simeon ben Jochai (circa 75 CE)—escaped from the besieged Jerusalem and concealed himself in a cave where he stayed for twelve years. While in exile, he wrote down for the first time, the "Oral Tradition" of Kabbalah.

Rakiah—sky or barrier in Genesis existing between the waters above and below.

Raphael—"Healing of God"; Archangel associated with Sephira Tiphereth and the Sun.

Rephaim—phantoms.

Resha-havurah—the "White Head" from which flows the fiery fluid of life and intelligence. It moves in three hundred and seventy streams throughout the Universe.

Rashith—"beginning".

Raziel—Archangel associated with Sephira Chokmah and the Zodiac.

Rimmon—a Pomegranate; the type of abundant fertility mentioned in the Old Testament; an emblem of the celestial Mother of all.

Ruach—"Spirit" or "the seat of spiritual discernment"; aspect of the Soul making decisions using the intellect; symbolized by six Sephirot (four through nine); our reasoning powers which lie between the immortal Neshamah above, and the mortal Nephesh below.

Ruach-Elohim—Spirit of the Gods.

Ruach-ha-Kodesh—Divine Spirit.

S

Samael—"poison of God"; Prince of evil spirits; Angel of death.

Sandalphon—Archangel associated with Sephira Malkuth; Prince of Angels; represented by a Cherubim on the Ark of the Covenant.

Saphar—Sepharim; Sepher, Saphar or Sipur, or Number, Numbers and Numbered by whose unfoldment the world was formed.

Seraph—a flying serpent.

Sarah—wife of Abraham in the Old Testament.

Sarai—original name of the wife of Abram (Abraham).

Sepher Yetzirah—The Book of Formation; an ancient Kabbalistic text ascribed to Abraham. It illustrates the creation of the Universe by analogy with ten Sephirot and twenty-two letters of the Hebrew alphabet. It tells the story of the unfoldment of the Godhead and the Universe.

Sephira—"Sacred Aged"; one of ten divine emanations represented by a sphere on the Tree of Life.

Sephirot—the ten divine attributes emanating from Ain-Soph-Aur, the Limitless Light. Each Sephira spills over to form another

Sephira which has its own distinct divine qualities.

Sekhel—"intelligence"; states of consciousness associated with each of the 32 Paths of Wisdom on the Tree of Life.

Sepher—"book".

Sepher Dzeniouta (Dtzenioutha)—*Book of Concealed Mystery* found in the *Zohar*.

Seraphim (Serafim)—celestial beings described by Isaiah as having human form with the addition of three pairs of wings.

Shanah—the lunar year.

Shekinah—feminine potency of God; the Divine Presence of God in matter; the final Hé of the Tetragrammaton.

Shells—see Qlippoth.

Shem ha-Mephorash (Hamphorash)—the Ineffable Name of God; the Tetragrammaton; 72 Names of God.

Shemesh—the Sun.

Shemittot—great cosmic cycles.

Sheol—a region of stillness and inactivity; sometimes referred to as Hell.

Siddim—"pourers forth"; evil powers.

Sod—a religious mystery.

Solomon's Seal—the symbolic double triangle. The upward or downward direction determines its meaning. The upward triangle symbolizes the male element and divine fire. The downward triangle symbolizes the female element and the waters of matter.

T

Tab-nnoth—"form".

Tachutonim—"those who dwell here below"; inhabitants of Assiah.

Tahor—the world as relating to Pantheism.

Talmidai-Hakhameem—"Disciples of the Wise," as stated in the *Zohar;* a class of Kabbalistic mystics.

Talmud—the unwritten or Oral Law; Rabbinical commentaries about Judaism which is composed of two parts: the older *Mishnah,* and the more modern *Gemara.*

Tanakh—the Jewish Bible; includes the Pentateuch (Five Books of Moses), Nevi'im (Prophets) and Ketuvim (Writings).

Tebah—Nature; mystically and esoterically the personified Elohim.

Tehom—"the Deep"; the Abyss.

Temura—"change"; a system of transposition of letters and analogies between words.

Teraphim—same as Seraphim or serpent images.

Teshuvah—"Redemption"; a completed cycle of Creation. The return and ascent to the Divine source of origin.

Tetragrammaton—The four-lettered Ineffable name of God: YHVH; Yod-Hé-Vau-Hé; the true ancient pronunciation is unknown today. Sometimes, the title "Adonai" is used as a substitute, meaning Lord.

Theiohel—the Earth in the *Zohar.*

Thirty-Two Paths of Wisdom—The *Zohar* says, "Chokmah generates all things by means of these thirty-two paths." The full account is told in the *Sepher Yetzirah* whereby letters and numbers constitute the thirty-two paths. It is said that the brain, "hath an outlet from Zeir Anpin, and therefore, it spreads out in thirty-two ways." Zeir Anpin is the "Short Face," or "Lower Countenance." Man in the *Zohar* is looked upon as twenty-two letters of the Hebrew alphabet plus the ten Sephirot for a total of thirty-two symbols of man's spiritual, emotional and physical nature.

Thummim—"Perfections"; an ornament on the breastplates of the ancient High Priests of Judaism.

Tiphereth—"Beauty and Mildness"; the sixth Sephira corresponding to Vau or V of the Tetragrammaton.

Tohu (Bohu)—"the Deep"; primeval space; confusion and chaos before the Creation.

Tophet—a place in the valley of Gehenna near Jerusalem where a constant fire was burning and sacrifices took place. It was the prototype for Hell.

Torah—law; the Pentateuch or Five Books of Moses.

Triad—The Tree of Life is explained as a group of three triads: Keter, Chokmah and Binah form the Supernal Triad. Chesed, Geburah and Tiphereth form the second and Netzach, Hod and Yesod form the third. The tenth Sephira, Malkuth, is beyond the three triads.

Tzaila—a "rib"; Adam's rib which created the first woman in Genesis.

Tzaddik—a righteous, altruistic, unselfish person who performs good deeds or Mitzvot.

Tzadkiel—"God's Justice"; Archangel associated with the Sephira Chesed.

Tzaphkiel (Tsaphqiel)—Archangel associated with Binah.

Tzelem—an image; a shadow; garment of the Soul.

Tzim-Tzum—expansion and contraction; God created the Universe by expanding and contracting his own essence.

Tziruph—a mode of divination by Temura, or permutation of letters; it was taught by medieval Kabbalists such as Rabbis Abulafia and Gikatilla.

Tzuddakah—charity or giving of oneself without expectation of anything in return.

Tzurah (pl. Tzurath)—a divine prototype for the eternal Supernal triad; corresponds to Keter, Chokmah and Binah in Man.

U

Ur—ancient Chaldean city; birthplace of Abraham; light or moon city.

Uriel—"Fire of God"; Archangel who wrestled with Jacob in the desert; associated with Sephira Netzach.

Uzza—an Angel who (together with Azrael), opposed the creation of man by the Elohim.

V

Vale of Tears—The Fourth World of Expression or Assiah; the Soul is reluctant to return to the Earth, but God says, "It was for this that you were called, created, formed, and made."

Vau (Vav)—the sixth Hebrew letter; third letter of the Tetragrammaton, symbolizes the Son; associated with the third World of Yetzirah; symbol of Taurus; Path 16 on the Tree of Life.

W

White Fire—The *Zohar* speaks of "the Long Face" and "the Short Face" which are symbols of the Macrocosm and the Microcosm. The hidden White Fire corresponds to electricity on the higher and lower planes; mystically, another name for Ain-Soph.

Wisdom—the Kabbalists say, "the very essence of wisdom is contained in Non-Being." "The Principle of all Principles, the mysterious Wisdom, the crown of all there is of the most High."

Worlds (Inferior and Superior)—according to the *Zohar*, "the Inferior World of the lower seven Sephirot is but a reflection of the Superior World of the three highest Sephirot."

Y

Yah—as stated in the *Zohar*, the "Word" through which the Elohim formed the worlds; divine name associated with Chokmah.

Yahweh—the traditional name of God in Judaism. The Tetragrammaton—YHVH; the Lord.

Yechidah—the divine spiritual essence of Neshamah; highest aspect of the Soul; corresponds to the Sephira Keter.

Yesh—existence.

Yesod—"Foundation or Formation"; the ninth Sephira.

Yetzirah—the "Third World of "Formation"; the Angelic World; associated with the Vau of the Tetragrammaton; the *Sepher Yetzirah* is the Book of Formation.

YHVH—Yod-Hé-Vau-Hé; the Tetragrammaton or Ineffable name of God; these four Hebrew letters symbolize the Father, Mother, Son and Bride; pronounced Yahweh, Yahveh or Jahovah; associated with the Four Worlds of Existence. Y—Atziluth, H—Briah, V—Yetzirah and final H—Assiah; sometimes, "Adonai" is used as a substitute name.

Yod—the tenth letter of the Hebrew alphabet; first letter of the Tetragrammaton, symbolizes the Father; associated with the first World of Atziluth; symbol of Virgo; Path 20 on the Tree of Life.

Z

Zahzahoth—"hidden splendors"; three principles governing the ten Sephirot: Will, Justice, and Mercy.

Zeir (Zauir) Anpin—the Lesser Countenance; Microprospus; associated with Tiphereth.

Zelem—see Tzelem.

Zohar—"splendor"; the Book of Splendor, circa 1285. First appeared in Spain in the late thirteenth century. The most influential work in Kabbalah. Scholars attribute its authorship to Moses de Leon. Treatises in the *Zohar* include, *The Hidden Midrash, The Mysteries of the Pentateuch, The Mansions and Abodes of Paradise and Gaihinnom, The Faithful Shepherd, The Secret of Secrets, Discourse of the Aged Mishpatim, The Januka or Discourse of the Young Man, The Book of Concealed Mystery, The Book of the Greater Holy Assembly* and *The Book of the Lesser Holy Assembly.*

Bob Waxman (Neer Aish-Donag) was a student of Rabbi Azriel Abraham of Jerusalem from 1985–1998, He co-hosted the national radio show, *Spiritually Speaking*, and has appeared on the national media to explain the essential teachings of Kabbalah.

Bob blends Kabbalistic wisdom and spiritual common sense into an innovative blueprint for personal transformation and spiritual illumination. He explains the scholarly writings of Gershom Scholem, Aryeh Kaplan and Isaiah Tishby in an easy to understand and entertaining manner.

Bob is a frequent guest speaker at universities, synagogues, Jewish Community Centers, bookstores, adult learning centers, religious conferences and many other philosophical and religious organizations. He is also a founding member of "The International Kabbalah Association." Bob teaches at The Education Center and has been facilitating Kabbalah classes on the east and west coasts of Florida since 1998. He is also a graduate of The American Seminar Leaders Association.

All discussion topics for his classes include scholarly insights into the three primary Kabbalistic texts: the *Sepher Yetzirah*, the *Sepher Ha-Bahir* and the *Zohar*.

Rabbi Azriel Abraham (1902-1998) taught and lectured throughout Israel on a wide range of topics explaining the Torah, Kavannah (mystical meditation) and Kabbalah. He participated in single lectures, lecture series, seminars, special activities for professionals, teacher supplementary study programs, rabbinical schools, yeshivot, cultural centers and kibbutzim. Rabbi Azriel Abraham combined his talent for speech, his unique Torah knowledge and his rich and varied experiences to captivate his audiences with a strong connection between science, Kabbalistic mysticism and ancient symbology. He had a deep knowledge of many other fields, among them physics, psychology, musical orchestration, meditation and philosophy. He integrated this rich background into his lectures and connected all these different fields with Kabbalah and Torah.